£4

Modern Music Masters Paul Weller

The Solo Years

Tom Boniface-Webb

Modern Music Masters

ISBN: 978-1-8381887-7-1
modernmusicmastersuk@gmail.com

DEDICATION

This book is dedicated to another Modfather, my old man, Chris Webb, who first introduced me to the incredible music of Paul Weller.

CONTENTS

Acknowledgments i

- Preface 1
- Foreword 3
- A few words from the author 7

1 Weller's career so far – Woking to London, The Jam to The Style Council (1958-1990) 11

2 Into Tomorrow – *Paul Weller* (1990-1992) 19

3 The Imperial Phase – *Wild Wood, Live Wood* and *Stanley Road* (1993-1996) 31

4 The Island Years pt. 1 – *Heavy Soul, Modern Classics and Heliocentric* (1996-2000) 59

5 Independiente – *Days of Speed, Illumination* and *Fly on the Wall: B Sides & Rarities* (2001-2003) 83

6 *Studio 150, As Is Now, Catch-Flame!* and *Hit Parade* (2004-2007) 98

7 The Island Years pt. 2 – *22 Dreams, Weller at the BBC,* and *Wake Up the Nation* (2008-2010) 122

8 *Find the Torch, Burn the Plans – Live at the Royal Albert Hall, Sonik Kicks* and *More Modern Classics* (2011-2014) 146

9 The Parlophone Years – *Saturns Pattern, A Kind Revolution, True Meanings* and *Other Aspects – Live at the Royal Festival Hall* (2015-2019) 162

10 Weller Under Lockdown – *On Sunset* and *Fat Pop (Volume 1)* (2020-2021) 179

- About the Author 193

- Endnotes 194

n.b. all songs written by Paul Weller unless otherwise stated

ACKNOWLEDGMENTS

Thank you to all the following, without whom this book would not have been possible:

Cover Design: Barry Parkinson at www.beepea.co.uk
www.discogs.com
Martin Talbot, Chief Executive, Official Charts Company
Rob Poole, Commercial Manager, Official Charts Company

The Modern Music Masters series is now published in partnership with the UK Official Charts Company.

Books in the Modern Music Masters Series:

Oasis
Blur
Pulp
Manic Street Preachers
The Verve
Suede
Paul Weller – The Solo Years

MMM7 – Paul Weller Spotify Playlist

Available at: MMM7 – Weller – Solo

PREFACE:

Welcome to this latest volume of *Modern Music Masters*, a series of books chronicling the stories behind many of the UK's favourite music artists and which are supported by the Official Charts Company.

This volume focusses on the incredible musical contribution made by the Modfather himself, Paul Weller and follows past publications focussing on the likes of Blur, Oasis, Pulp and Suede. Like its predecessors, it tells the former frontman of The Jam's fascinating story over the past three decades in the context of his chart history as a solo artist.

The Official Charts have been chronicling British public's love of music over eight different decades now, from the Fifties right through to the current day. And, in doing so, they have reflected the way that music is consumed and listened to in many different ways, from 78 RPM discs in the Fifties right through to the streaming services of today.

As well as being the ultimate reflection of music fandom, the Official Charts – both singles and albums – are one of the few places where artists can take on their peers every week, and reflect the evolution of their careers, the highs and lows, through their Number 1s, their Top 10s and the chart positions they might rather forget. That is the same today as it has ever been.

We hope you enjoy tracing the journeys of these musical icons, through the Official Charts and beyond.

Martin Talbot
Chief Executive, Official Charts Company
November 2021

FOREWORD:

So, what do we think of when we think of Paul Weller? The Modfather himself. Unlike any of the other artists featured in the MMM series so far (apart from perhaps Damon Albarn), no other act is as prolific as Paul Weller, and none has a story that is so intrinsically tied together with their music. Weller simply lives and breathes music, there are very few artists that have an artform so deeply ingrained into their soul as he does.

First appearing on the music scene as the leader of pop power trio, The Jam, punk provided the perfect vitriolic vehicle for Weller to announce his arrival on the UK music scene. After six albums over five years, his second incarnation couldn't have been further removed from mod-punk stylings of The Jam if he had tried (which he did), and the eclectic blue-eyed-soul modernism of The Style Council, struck a chord with the eighties rejection of all past eras.

But it is the third period of his musical life that this book is interested in. To be a solo artist can be a tough hand to play. You bear the weight of the whole musical act, and its criticism, both good and bad, rests solely on your shoulders. The Beatles were able to share the burden of being the world's biggest band, which kept them grounded, whilst Elvis didn't have that luxury. So surrounded was he by sycophants, that toward the end, he was unable to tell the difference between the truth and the smoke being blown up his behind. Somehow, Paul Weller has managed to ride that almost impossible line between autocratic genius and collaborative artist without slipping too far into either camp. Perhaps by surrounding himself with those that would always speak truth to power (his plain speaking father John, his manager for many years, would always make sure to put Paul in his place), or by playing with the same musicians for an extended period of time (Steve Cradock has played guitar on nearly every single one of his solo albums), he has managed to keep his head when many artists around him have lost theirs.

Due to the huge output of material, this has been the hardest entry in the series to write so far. Weller has released sixteen studio albums to date, plus seven live albums, five best-ofs, a film soundtrack and 68 singles, all in the space of 30 years. It's an incredible output, but one that has only grown more and more rich over time. I have tried to give space to all his albums equally, whilst also remaining honourable to the brevity of the series. But, for a more in-depth look at Weller's work, you may wish to refer to his good friend Paolo Hewitt's biography, told through a selection of key songs, *The Changing Man* (Penguin, 2011); or Ian Snowball's excellent analysis of every track on every Weller album (up to 2015's *Saturns Pattern*), *Paul Weller: Sounds from the Studio* (This Day in Music Books, 2020), to which I am truly indebted with this book. I also referred to many print and online magazines for reviews and articles, including *The Guardian*, the *NME*, and in particular, the June 2021 edition of *Mojo*, edited by the man himself, Mr Paul Weller.

Although the MMM series has always drawn heavily from the UK Official Charts Company database, this is the first book in the series to be published in official partnership with them. I have always considered the chart focus of the series to be its USP, and such a partnership heralds a marrying of minds to which I am hugely proud, and grateful.

There will be future books in the *Modern Music Masters* series, as always, stay tuned to find out what will be up next, but for the moment, sit back and enjoy *Modern Music Masters – Paul Weller – The Solo Years*. I hope you enjoy it.

Tom Boniface-Webb
November 2021

A FEW WORDS FROM THE AUTHOR

My first memory of Paul Weller is hard to pin down. Having been born in 1981, his music with The Jam and then The Style Council was a constant part of the general cultural fabric of my upbringing. As a teenager, delving into The Style Council back catalogue, I was amazed to find the likes of You're the Best Thing and Shout to the Top so familiar, having clearly heard them on the radio, or at my parents' parties, when I was a kid. And so, just like The Beatles, the Stones and the Who, it is almost impossible to consider what Paul Weller means to me as an artist, because his music has always been there.

Except, at the same time, it's not that hard to consider, because I also became aware of Weller as a solo artist around the time of Britpop. He reinvented himself in the early nineties, the era that I came of age in musically, and in essence began his whole career again. He is in a very small group of artists, alongside such exalted company as George Michael, Sting and Phil Collins, whose solo careers are more successful than the bands they first found success in.

Anyone familiar to the *Modern Music Masters* series will know that I fell for Oasis in a big way, and along with following the path back to The Beatles, I was happy to discover that one of Noel Gallagher's biggest influences as a songwriter was not only still around but leading the charge with some incredible new music. *Stanley Road* did it for me, the combination of the retro-cool Broken Stones, the heartfelt beauty of You Do Something to Me, combined with the omnipresence of The Changingman and Out of the Sinking on the radio, and on *Shine* and the *Best Album in the World...Ever!* compilations, positioned the album as one of my favourites of 1995. And the fact he had John Lennon on the album cover made the whole thing a lot more intriguing.

Then, when he popped up as one third of the Smokin' Mojo Filters, alongside not only Noel Gallagher but also Sir Paul McCartney, covering The Beatles' Come Together for *The Help Album* in September 1995, it was clear this guy was someone I needed to get to know more.

After my parents split up when I was 16, I moved in with my father, and music helped us connect. We bonded over *Heavy Soul*, and this book is dedicated to him for helping me discover Weller's music. In 1997 I bought *The Very Best of The Jam* (released in October 1997) from the Sound Machine in Reading (remember, this is a long time before *Spotify*), which opened my eyes to a whole new world of Weller's music. I couldn't be there at the 100 Club in 1977, but the pace and passion of the songs kept the spirit alive, and before long I had collected everything The Jam had released in the incredibly short period of time they were together, also veering off into The Kinks back catalogue via The Jam's version of David Watts. Such is the beauty and joined-up nature of popular music.

In 1999, *Fire & Skill: The Songs of the Jam*, was released on Ignition Records, Marcus Russell's (manager of Oasis) label, and featured contemporary artists covering songs by The Jam. Liam Gallagher and Steve Cradock did Carnation, The Beastie Boys did Start!, Garbage did The Butterfly Collector and Noel Gallagher did a passionate version of To Be Someone. The album failed to chart, mostly probably because its audience was so niche, but to me it signalled both the lasting legacy of the band, and Weller's skill as a songwriter.

I never really got into The Style Council though, until more recently they seemed incredibly uncool, despite the quality and familiarity of their songs. This is partly the reason that Weller found launching his solo career such a challenge. It was certainly never a fait accompli and turning the tide of popular opinion back after the final lost days of The Style Council, was just as hard as managing to sustain such a quality solo career for all this time.

But turn it back he did, and sustain it, he has. I kept up with Weller's releases over the years and saw him play at V Festival in 2000. It was not long after *Heliocentric* came out, and at the time it felt a little lacklustre, that his heart wasn't really in it anymore. *Days of Speed*, his 2001 live acoustic best-of album, made perfect sense to me, particularly the reference in the title to That's Entertainment, a song which I was desperately obsessed with at the time, and it felt for a while like he was drawing his solo career to a slow conclusion, looking back with retrospect over his years as an artist in order to wind things down.

Of course, today that seems ridiculous. With the release of *Illumination* in 2002, he was only really just getting things going, and when the covers album *Studio 150* came out in 2004, it felt like he was reinventing himself yet again. It is this constant reimagining of his music that keeps him so alive as an artist, keeping his sound fresh, as well as the constant stream of pop-hits, and when From the Floorboards Up was released as a single ahead of *As Is Now* in 2005, it was clear that Weller was positioning himself as the most current of artists.

After that, I, and the wider musical world, stopped guessing when or if Weller was going to wrap up his solo career, but rather, began to tune in expectantly for whatever it was he was going to do next. The idea of the double album *22 Dreams* seemed overblown and bordering on pretentious, but it sounded fantastic, yet again proving there was another angle to his work. Another live album – sounds great; another best-of – need to hear those hits again; an acoustic album – I'm sure it'll be very heartfelt; an orchestral live retelling of his latest studio album – why the hell not.

It all adds up to the rich tapestry of one fascinating story through time and music. I just hope that my 45,000 words on Weller's last 30 years are able to capture just one tiny amount of what he, as an artist, means to the world.

CHAPTER ONE
Weller's Career So Far, Woking To London, The Jam to The Style Council (1958-1990)

Born John William on 25th May 1958, Weller became known as Paul because his father was also John, so was named, at his own insistence, after his favourite Beatle, Paul McCartney. Although he was only 12 when the Fab Four split in 1970, they always loomed large in Weller's musical education. As he was growing up, their music was so ubiquitous it felt like the ambient sound of the very time and place it was produced, synonymous then and today with the very word: sixties.

Unlike today though, an era in which The Beatles are so cemented into British musical history to be impervious to bucking trends, as the seventies wore on, they became more and more unfashionable. A point made solid when punk heroes The Clash immortalised their feelings in their 1979 era-defining single London Calling: "Phoney Beatlemania has bitten the dust".

So, although Weller and The Jam came of age amongst the leather jackets and spit stains of the punk era, allying themselves to it, and found their early success as part of it, their mod suits and floppy hair gave them a retro image that they used to define themselves. This helped them stand out from the other, well, dirtier, punk groups. The image worked so well that it has never strayed far from how Weller is seen by the British music industry, eventually earning him the title of the Modfather, but only once he was old enough to wear it properly.

Weller has continued to fuel his close association with mod culture and modernism, purposefully keeping the flame burning for the many fallen musical heroes who helped define his own music – Steve Marriott, Ronnie Lane, Brian Jones, Keith Moon, John Lennon – and despite the shifting sands of fashion time inevitably draws. In many ways it could be said that the mod association keeps his tastes limited and retrospective – he professes a hatred for all seventies rock bands like Led Zeppelin, for example – but it means that he has gone deep into his subject area and become an expert in soul, early rock 'n' roll, and the original R&B, obsessed with the sixties and seventies, in the same way that Martin Scorsese is an expert in gangster films.

Today there are few people as committed to their subject area as he, and youngsters discovering music can use his example to springboard back into music history like few other contemporary artists.

Take the CD he included with the edition of Mojo he edited in June 2021 – the aptly named *Into Tomorrow* – for example. New tracks by contemporary R&B and soul acts like Durand Jones & The Indications, Black Pumas, or The Stone Foundation (who Weller also collaborated with), sit alongside new tracks from classic artists like The Blow Monkeys, PP Arnold and Weller himself, to give a little insight into what Weller was listening to that time. The style may be limited, but he keeps up to date with new music, and you get an array of amazing tracks you might not have come across otherwise.

In the City There Are a Thousand Things I Want to Say to You

The Jam found its origins in the commuter-belt town of Woking, Surrey, in 1972, when Weller was just 14 years old. After the requisite shuffling about, the band settled on the classic line-up of Weller on guitar and vocals, Bruce Foxton on bass and vocals, and Rick Buckler on drums, in about 1975. After playing some blistering gigs in London they caught the eye of Chris Parry at Polydor, who they signed with in early 1977. Legend has it that Weller threatened to give away the £6,000 (£33k today), he was personally paid as an advance to stick to his punk roots, but his father (and manager) hit the roof when he found out.

They supported The Clash on the infamous *White Riot Tour* after the release of Strummer et al's eponymous debut album in April 1977, their age, energy and volume making them quickly popular live with the punks, and their debut single In the City reached number 40 in May that same year. The accompanying album of the same name went to number 20 three weeks later, a month before The Sex Pistols released God Save the Queen and punk went mainstream proper.

Weller and The Jam were careful not to ally themselves too closely with punk though and although their second album, *This is the Modern World*, shared its predecessor's energy, aggression and lyrics about disenfranchised youth, Weller shocked his audience by telling the *NME* in 1977 he was going to vote for Margaret Thatcher's Tory party at the next general election. In a country led by a failing Labour government, who seemed to be rejecting the youth more than any for a generation, it was perhaps a protest statement designed to be provocative, and of course Weller had no idea what Thatcher had in store for the country and the working classes he was a proud member of once she got her hands on the keys to number 10.

Whatever his reasoning, the statement has clung to Weller throughout his entire career despite him saying two years later, with Thatcher poised to take over as Prime Minister, that he was not political, telling *Jamming* magazine he didn't think he was clever enough. Considering the political impact of some of his most well-known songs, Going Underground and its anti-nuclear war message in particular, and That's Entertainment, with its sad story of misery in poverty, it's ironic that Weller would make such a statement about politics in 1979.

As it would transpire, Weller would eventually become one of the key figures of his era in left wing politics and, alongside Billy Bragg, he played a key part in the formation of Red Wedge in 1985, an organisation formed to combat the apathy youngsters often felt about politics, just as Weller had shown signs of six years earlier. Considering their key aim was to oust Thatcher from power at the 1987 general election, Red Wedge ultimately failed, with the Tories claiming a third successive landslide victory, although turnout did increase by 2.6%, and Labour experienced a 3.2% swing in their favour (20 extra seats gained). Perhaps Bragg and Weller were responsible.

By the time The Jam released their quintessential long player *All Mod Cons* in November 1978, punk figure heads The Sex Pistols were no more, Sid Vicious' tragic self-inflicted death in February 1979 drawing an unofficial line under punk and reducing but not eradicating its weighty impact on popular culture in Britain. By May, Thatcher's Tory party would scrape to victory at the polls, and the long arduous slog of the eighties would begin.

Weller would soon become one of the key dissenting popular culture voices throughout the long decade, which quickly became mired by war, strikes, protests, mass-scale unemployment and one of the worst diseases the world had ever seen: AIDS. As the decade got under way, Weller would continue to pen songs about youth experiences, the misery of small-town life, love, loss, betrayal, and poverty; whilst his song about the fear of nuclear holocaust, Going Underground (his first number 1, in March 1980), made him the unwitting spokesman for a generation, terrified, like so many other youngsters were, to come of age in a decade that showed such clear disdain for the working classes.

After a string of hit singles, including four number 1s, and a number 1 album, *The Gift* in March 1982, Weller surprised everyone – none more so than Foxton and Buckler – when he announced the split of The Jam in October 1982.

You're the Best Thing That Ever Happened

Following hot on the heels of The Bitterest Pill (I Ever Had to Swallow), a number 2 single in September, their last single Beat Surrender went to number 1 in November 1982, and one of the Britain's most important bands was no more. If anyone had noticed the soulful style of these two non-album singles, so distanced from the early pop-punk of In the City and All Around the World as to be two completely different bands, then The Jam's split may not have come as such a surprise. It had become clear that Weller's musical tastes were developing and the image he had played a major part in manufacturing of

The Jam, the one of young, energetic, bitter and discontented kids, was going to be at total odds with the new style of music he was interested in making.

Enter Mick Talbot and a new band, which soon became known by the slightly mulchy name, The Style Council. Leaving little time for fans of The Jam to come to terms with the split, The Style Council were in a recording studio in February 1983, their first single Speak Like a Child reaching number 4 just three months after Beat Surrender, in March.

Where northern soul brought the influence of American soul and R&B to the shores of Britain, inserting an amphetamine-led energy to the famous all-nighters, The Style Council took the Detroit sound of Motown Records and added their own set of London-based influences: Nell Dunn novels, their subsequent Ken Loach TV adaptations, Tony Hancock and George Orwell, wrapping them up in a neat little blue-eyed soul package, seemingly at total odds with their subject matter.

It wasn't a new idea, Weller had purposefully lifted the bass-riff from The Supremes' You Can't Hurry Love for The Jam's anthem Town Called Malice, topping the singles chart in February 1982, in just the same way he had also lifted the bass-riff from The Beatles' Taxman for another chart topper, Start!, in August 1980. It was as an homage, rather than a rip-off, and as it turns out, he had been laying the seeds for his obsession with soul and Motown which The Style Council would directly lift influence from.

Things started well for Weller's new outfit. Their debut album *Café Bleu* reached number 2 in March 1984, its follow-up *Our Favourite Shop* went to number 1 in June 1985, and some of those early singles, notably You're the Best Thing, Shout to the Top!, and Walls Come Tumbling Down, rank among some of the best pop tracks that Weller has ever written. But the journey was not the same as The Jam, and rather than the work becoming stronger and more popular as the band's experience grew, the opposite seemed to be the case.

As Mick Talbot said to Mojo in June 2021, the writing was on the wall the whole time: "The beginning of the end? I suppose we kind of lost a lot of people with *The Cost of Loving* [number 2 album in February 1987]. We knew we could have done another *Our Favourite Shop*, but it wasn't what we'd done. We'd never made the same record twice."[i]

The cost of innovation, of never revisiting the same sound twice, became apparent on the aptly named *Confessions of a Pop Group*, their fourth studio album, which reached an unflattering number 15 in June 1988. It was Weller's lowest charting album since *This is the Modern World*, way back in November 1977 and, interestingly enough, he has never had a studio album chart as low in the 33 years since.

The band may have believed in the record, but The Style Council disbanded in 1989 after their fifth and final album, *Modernism: A New Decade*, their attempt at house music, was rejected by their label, Polydor. The album finally got a release in 1998, when Weller was at the height of his solo career, limping to a not-great number 100 in the albums chart, as part of *The Complete Adventures of The Style Council*, a box set for the real hardcore.

Never quite gaining the lasting reputation of The Jam or the longevity of Weller's solo career, The Style Council were incredibly unfashionable throughout the nineties, but have managed to gain some kind of historical footing subsequentially, with seven best-ofs released since their split, the most recent *Long*

Hot Summers – The Story of The Style Council, reaching a promising number 8, in November 2020.

So, as Weller finally began to consider a solo career as the nineties – the decade that in many ways would come to define him as a musician – began, there was no surety at all that it would work out. The Jam were long gone, The Style Council quickly forgotten, he had no record deal, and the country was in the grip of acid house, The Stone Roses and Happy Mondays' fever, a sound that could not have been further from Weller's mod roots if it had tried. The Stone Roses may have started out as a scooter gang, necking amphetamines at northern soul all-nighters, but the drum loops and synths evident on Fools Gold and One Love held little interest to the now 32-year-old Weller. Whilst getting his band together, drummer Steve White agreed to join as long as there were "no fucking drum loops!"

As it turned out, it would be two years before his first solo album appeared and a further year for him to properly work out what his solo career was going to sound like. But, when it finally clicked, not only would his original audience prove themselves loyal and desperate to hear what he would come up with next, he would find a whole new one in the Britpop years, an era that fit Weller as well as an old parka that had been lurking at the back of his wardrobe. And with it would come some of the best tracks that he would ever write.

CHAPTER TWO
Into Tomorrow – *Paul Weller* (1990-1992)

With no interest from Polydor, Weller launched his solo career with his own label, Freedom High. He had been married to The Style Council backing singer Dee C. Lee since 1987, and by the time of the release of his debut solo album in 1992, the pair had two children, Leah and Nathaniel.

Weller was a family man. He turned 33 just as his debut solo single was released, and it was clear that the angry young man who had spat out, "I wanna tell you, about the young ideas, but you turn them into fears" on In The City in 1977, was now grown up, and his music needed to be more mature if it was going to connect with its audience in the same way. The album that Weller would name after himself would press the reset button, and do just that.

Weller began his solo career with a string of relatively small gigs throughout November and December 1990, playing the likes of Dingwalls in Camden, the Manchester Academy, and a run of university gigs throughout England, Wales, Northern Ireland and Scotland. The gigs were not particularly well attended, but by keeping things low-key, Weller managed to cut his teeth with his new band and slowly build his confidence whilst working out what his solo career was going to look and sound like. He hadn't stopped writing or working on new material, but after the demise of the Style Council, and being dropped by Polydor, his confidence with his song writing had certainly been shaken, and he needed to start from the floorboards up.

He began by getting a band together, beginning with his long-term percussive collaborator Steve White, who had played drums for The Style Council and would stick with Weller throughout the heights of his solo career and well into the next century.

Debut Single

By February 1991 Weller and producer Brendan Lynch, who had worked on the lost Style Council album *Modernism*, found themselves ensconced in Weller's Solid Bond Studios in Central London, forced to stay put due to bad weather and so afforded the opportunity of really going to town on what would become Weller's debut solo single, the aptly named Into Tomorrow. The single was released completely on Weller's dime in May 1991, reaching a not-too-bad, number 36.

Single 1:

Into Tomorrow*
Released: 6th May 1991**; UK Chart Position: 36; Label: Freedom High; Album: *Paul Weller*
B-sides: Here's A New Thing; That Spiritual Feeling; Into Tomorrow (Original 8 Track Demo)

*released as the Paul Weller Movement
**the single did not chart until its second week of release on 12th May

Picking out the best bits of what made The Jam and the Style Council so exciting, including the former's energy and tunefulness and the latter's soulful leanings, Weller's debut solo single announced his return to the scene with a brass-tinged fanfare, a Hammond organ, backing vocals from the missus, and a prominent bass riff, the whole thing underpinned by Weller's distinct blue-eyed soul voice, really starting to come into its own.

Due in most part to the limited marketing and advertising spend, the single only just dented the top 40, but its impact was enough for Weller to be taken seriously by the industry again and Andy Macdonald soon reached out, signing him to Go! Discs in 1992. By this point the album had already been recorded, again, at Weller's own expense, so there was little risk for Macdonald, but it was a wise move none-the-less and began a fruitful and long-lasting relationship between record label and musician, one of the best of Weller's career.

<u>UK Official Singles Chart – Top 10 – 12th May 1991:</u>

1. The Shoop Shoop Song (It's in His Kiss) – Cher
2. Last Train to Trancentral – KLF ft. The Children of the Revolution
3. Gypsy Woman (La Da Dee) – Crystal Waters
4. Sailing in the Seven Seas – Orchestral Manoeuvres in the Dark
5. Touch Me (All Night Long) – Cathy Dennis
6. Promise Me – Beverley Craven
7. Senza Una Donna (Without a Woman) – Zucchero ft. Paul Young
8. There's No Other Way – Blur
9. Get the Message – Electronic
10. Tainted Love – Soft Cell ft. Marc Almond

…………………………………………………………

36. Into Tomorrow – The Paul Weller Movement

The world that Weller released Into Tomorrow into was awash with a mix of musical genres. Cher was at number 1 with the KLF at number 2, two incredibly different acts battling it out for the top spot; whilst signs of what was around the corner were evident in Blur's first hit single, There's No Other Way, creeping into the top 10 at number 8.

Manchester supergroup Electronic were also at number 9 with Get the Message, signalling the country's obsession with Madchester was far from over. Although, none of this was Weller's thing at all, and it would be something of a battle for him to wrestle the musical reigns back in his direction.

Big in Japan

Who could have guessed that a trip to Japan would help Weller find his solo feet?

Being big in Japan is something of a rock 'n' roll cliché. Rob Reiner chose to end his classic 1984 film *This is Spinal Tap* by giving the eponymous band a new lease of life in the far east, but in Weller's case, the cliché was true. The Paul Weller Movement went to Japan twice in the early days, once in November 1991 and then again in July 1992, and *Paul Weller* was even released via Pony Canyon in Japan in April 1992, six whole months earlier than its UK release. It went straight to number 1 in the Japanese charts. Weller was very appreciative of the part his Japanese fans played in his return to the charts. "Those gigs were me trying to find my feet," says Paul. "And I found my direction again."[ii]

Back in the UK and a mini tour of London, playing such places as the Clapham Grand and the Mean Fiddler as well as dates on the other side of the pond in New York, Chicago and LA, culminated in the release of his second solo single, the first to be released through Go! Discs, Uh Huh Oh Yeh!, which went top 20, peaking at number 18 in August 1992. Momentum was gathering for the solo project and the floor was being set for the release of the debut long player in September.

Single 2:

Uh Huh Oh Yeh!
Released: 9th August 1992; UK Chart Position: 18*; Label: Go! Discs; Album: *Paul Weller*
B-sides: Arrival Time; Fly on The Wall; Always There to Fool You

*the single reached its highest chart position in week two of its release

UK Official Singles Chart – Top 10 – 15th August 1992:

1. Rhythm is a Dancer – Snap!
2. Barcelona (1992) – Freddie Mercury and Montserrat Caballe
3. Achy Breaky Heart – Billy Ray Cyrus
4. The Best Things in Life are Free – Luther Vandross and Janet Jackson
5. Just Another Day – Jon Secada
6. Don't You Want Me – Felix
7. Ain't No Doubt – Jimmy Nail
8. This Charming Man (1992) – The Smiths
9. Baker Street – Undercover
10. Shake Your Head – Was (Not Was)

....

18. Uh Huh Oh Yeh! – Paul Weller

Featuring some long-lost classics such as The Best Things in Life are Free, a duet between Luther Vandross and Janet Jackson, the posthumous rerelease of Barcelona by Freddie Mercury in honour of the Olympic games, as well as the number 1 smash from Ol' Crocodile Shoes himself, Jimmy Nail, with Ain't No Doubt, summer 1992 in the charts was a typically varied affair.

It even featured a rerelease of This Charming Man by The Smiths, which peaked 17 spaces higher than first time around (nine years earlier) at number 8, signalling a return in interest to the Manchester miseries, led by the release of two new best ofs.

Debut Solo Long Player

Album 1:

Paul Weller
Released: 31st August 1992; UK Chart Position: 8; Label: Go! Discs
Track Listing: Uh-Huh Oh Yeh; I Didn't Mean to Hurt You; Bull Rush; Round & Round; Remember How We Started; Above the Clouds; Clues; Into Tomorrow; Amongst Butterflies; The Strange Museum (Paul Weller/Mick Talbot); Bitterness Rising; Kosmos
Producer/s: Paul Weller; Brendan Lynch

UK Official Albums Chart – Top 10 – 6th September 1992:

1. *Tubular Bells II* – Mike Oldfield
2. *Tourism* – Roxette
3. *Greatest Hits* – Kylie Minogue
4. *Back to Front* – Lionel Richie

5. *Diva* – Annie Lennox
6. *Unplugged* – Eric Clapton
7. *Best 1* – The Smiths
8. ***Paul Weller* – Paul Weller**
9. *The Greatest Hits 1966-1992* – Neil Diamond
10. *Dangerous* – Michael Jackson

A solo artist amongst a string of solo artists... and The Smiths and Roxette, is how the top 10 albums chart looked in September 1992. It was almost like a return to the highs of the singer-songwriter period of the early seventies. In fact, most of the albums that sat alongside Weller's return to form album were made by artists who had achieved most of their success in previous decades and were aiming for another bite of the apple ten years later, including Kylie Minogue, Lionel Richie, Michael Jackson, whilst Eric Clapton was doing just what Weller was trying, something new, this time an unplugged acoustic album which featured Tears in Heaven, arguably the best song written during his solo career.

The somewhat stale chart filled with best-ofs though points the finger squarely at unimaginative record labels, who would apparently rather stick out a greatest hits than invest any money in new music.

Paul Weller

Recording *Paul Weller* proved to be something of a labour of love – and a drain on the pocket – for Weller and Lynch. Aside from White, who plays on every song, the only other consistent musician is Paul himself, who plays guitar, bass, keyboards and of course, sings. Dr Robert, an old friend and leader of The Blow Monkeys, provides some support in the form of a bit of bass and a bit of backing vocals; whilst still clearly in the experimentation phase, Jacko Peake's saxophone is overly prominent, particularly on Round and Round, a decision that may have been regretted with hindsight. Mrs Weller leads a contingent of soulful backing singers, and it is these voices – rather than Peake's late-night jazz sax – that ultimately stand the course, becoming something of a Weller trademark, even on the down-the-line Brit-rock of *Stanley Road* and *Heavy Soul*.

It was clear that Weller was aiming for the album to be "'a mixture of the two things,' referring to The Jam and The Style Council"[iii], as he told Jonathan Ross in May 1991, but in aiming to fit somewhere in the middle, the album stumbles onto what will make Weller's solo career so special. A happy mid-point between his two musical projects, Weller solo doesn't alienate the young white males who listened to The Jam, nor the uber-soul boys and girls who were impressed by The Style Council. *Paul Weller* is at once classic and traditional in terms of sound and song writing style whilst clearly so in love with its own sense of tune and melody to appear fully new and original at the same time.

Always finding influence in the music he loves and contemporary music being released into the world around him, the lack of any real mainstream scene whilst the album was being written and recorded (grunge was in the process of breaking around the world, but such miserable music never would have crossed Weller's radar), gives it a sense of freedom that the records he released later in the nineties didn't have. As he began to release more albums, not only was he allied to the changing scenes going on around him, most prominently Britpop and his association with Oasis and Ocean Colour Scene, but also by the weight of his own back catalogue.

The success of *Stanley Road* would act as a double-edged sword for Weller. On the one hand, it was fantastic for him to be experiencing the type of success he had enjoyed during The Jam years, but it gave his music a yardstick against which all his future work would be judged. With the release of *Paul Weller,* he was in the enviable, but by no means secure, position of being afforded a second turn at pressing the reset button. The album would of course be judged with a view to his previous work, whilst also being looked at on its own terms, and for its own many merits.

Things began as they meant to go on with the release of Uh Huh Oh Yeh! (Always There to Fool You!), the second single from the album, an upbeat Motown inspired number that samples the brass refrain from soul singer Marsha Hunt's Hot Rod Poppa (written by Marc Bolan from T-Rex). Anecdotally, Hunt released Hot Rod Poppa in 1969 in France and Italy as a double A-side with Dr John's Walk on Gilded Splinters, which of course Weller would also cover on *Stanley Road*. Uh Huh is an upbeat number that immediately lets the listener know that the energy of The Jam was back, but now mixed with the introspection of The Style Council's tenure.

Paul Weller is predominantly an upbeat rock 'n' roll record, but I Didn't Mean to Hurt You is a mid-tempo soul ballad that owes not just a little to Nina Simone's Please Don't Let Me Be Misunderstood, the message of which permeates across the whole of the album. The album may be incredibly self-assured, but Weller must have been terrified that its sound and tone may not chime with its intended audience, just in the way the last few Style Council albums had missed their mark.

As history soon proved though, he needn't have been worried, and with each new track the album develops its own sense of self and purpose, returning Weller to the party which he had started back at the end of the seventies. Like the Style Council albums, there isn't as much lead guitar as we would become familiar with on his next three records, and aside from a handful of picked riffs and subtle solos, this is the one area that *Paul Weller* is too reliant on its influences (American soul and Motown) and not enough on its writer's own strengths. It is almost as if Weller has forgotten that he can play guitar. Although it's not all old school Detroit soul-rock, Bull-Rush has a backwards coda reminiscent of *Revolver* era Beatles.

All the material on the album was new, save for the excellently named The Strange Museum, another soul-flecked, electric-piano led slow ballad that Weller rescued from the cutting room floor of The Style Council's sessions. The song is an introspective number with no discernible chorus, but which rolls around and around, aptly representing the other side of the music that Weller is going to create in his solo work, the quieter, more reflective work. Similarly, he whips out the acoustic guitar on Bitterness Rising, suggesting where he is going to go with his next album *Wild Wood*.

An album highlight is the Marvin Gaye What's Going On-esque Above the Clouds. The track is slow and thoughtful, the backing track simple and functional, supporting lyrics that provides Weller's audience with a first look at the existential nature of his thoughts at the time:

As my anger shouts at my own self doubt
So a sadness creeps into my dreams
When you're scared of living but afraid to die
I get scared of giving and I must find the faith to beat it

The song remains a fan favourite, although its subtlety keeps it from properly entering Weller's greatest solo hits territory, and sadly the single version failed to enter the top 40 for the same reason. The album though succeeded where its best track may have failed, chiming with its audience and becoming a minor hit. There was no doubting it, Weller was back.

Single 3:

Above the Clouds
Released: 28th September 1992; UK Chart Position: 47; Label: Go! Discs; Album: *Paul Weller*
B-sides: Everything Has A Price to Pay; All Year Round; Feeling Alright (Dave Mason)

UK Official Singles Chart – Top 10 – 4th October 1992:

1. Ebeneezer Goode – The Shamen
2. It's My Life – Dr Alban
3. Sleeping Satellite – Tasmin Archer
4. End of the Road – Boyz II Men
5. Baker Street – Undercover
6. I'm Gonna Get You – Bizarre Inc. ft. Angie Brown
7. Iron Lion Zion – Bob Marley and the Wailers
8. My Destiny – Lionel Richie
9. My Name is Prince – Prince

10. Sentinel – Mike Oldfield

....

47. Above the Clouds – Paul Weller

Considering its love amongst Weller's fanbase today, it is something of a shame that Above the Clouds didn't reach any higher than number 47 in the charts in October 1992, although the gentle introspective nature of the song was somewhat out of sorts with what else was going on at the time.

Part dance classic/part novelty hit Ebeneezer Goode ("e's are good, e's are good") at number 1 and It's My Life at number 2 signalled a double header of Britain's love for house music and how it had crossed over into the mainstream.

Alongside the likes of Lionel Richie, Prince, and even a posthumous hit for Bob Marley, there was little place for someone like Weller. But as the next few years would tell, that was all about to change.

CHAPTER THREE
The Imperial Phase – *Wild Wood, Live Wood* and *Stanley Road* (1993-1996)

The revitalised Weller had no intention of resting on his laurels and with the solo career in full swing the next few years became a blur of activity, writing, recording, releasing and touring some of his best known and most well-loved songs. This included *Wild Wood* and *Stanley Road*, two albums which, in many ways, came to define him as a solo artist.

After a few months off at the beginning of 1993, Weller was back out on the road in March, playing a handful of UK dates before leaping across the Atlantic once more to play North America, returning to the UK at the end of March and heading straight into the studio in April and May to record what would become *Wild Wood*.

When the album was released in September 1993, Weller and the band, which by then consisted of White on drums, semi-permanent bassist Yolanda Charles, Ocean Colour Scene's guitarist Steve Craddock on second guitar and Helen Turner on keys, plus a rolling make-up of extra musicians, embarked on the biggest tour to date.

They took in dates around the UK[iv], at Weller's home from home Japan, plus on into Germany, the US and Spain, before releasing a live version of the show, *Live Wood*, which was recorded predominantly at the Royal Albert Hall on 22nd November 1993 and the Wolverhampton Civic Hall on 9th March 1994. The success of the tour and the album, which went to number 13 in September 1994, proved that live, Weller was a formidable force and after all those years having been seen to lose his touch, was finally coming back into own.

Second Album

Recorded at The Manor Studios in Oxfordshire with Brendan Lynch again helming the control desk, the first signs of what *Wild Wood* would sound like came in the form of Weller's next single, Sunflower, released in July 1993, two months before the album. Sunflower is classic Weller, with a strong arpeggio guitar lick that sits under the chorus and signalled his desire to return to using the instrument that had made his name in the seventies.

Single 4:

Sunflower
Released: 5th July 1993; UK Chart Position: 16; Label: Go! Discs; Album: *Wild Wood*
B-sides: Kosmos SXDub 2000; Bull-Rush/Magic Bus (Weller/Townsend); That Spiritual Feeling [New Mix] (Weller/Mick Talbot/Dee C. Lee/Mark Alan Nelson)

UK Official Singles Chart – Top 10 – 11th July 1993:

1. Pray – Take That
2. Dreams – Gabrielle
3. What is Love – Haddaway
4. Tease Me – Chaka Demus and Pliers
5. What's Up – 4 Non Blondes
6. One Night in Heaven – M People
7. I Will Survive (1993) – Gloria Gaynor

8. (I Can't Help) Falling in Love With You – UB40
9. Will You Be There – Michael Jackson
10. Have I Told You Lately – Rod Stewart
………………………………………..
16. Sunflower – Paul Weller

The one thing that all the songs in the top 10 had in common, during the week that Sunflower went to number 16, is that none of them were the guitar driven rock 'n' roll that Weller was attempting to bring back to the charts. Which is no real surprise, considering the man himself had barely touched the instrument since the late seventies.

Aside from that though, there is little that Take That, Gabrielle and Chaka Demus and Pliers had in common other than their proximity to each other in the top 10.

The likes of Gloria Gaynor and the return of her seventies anthem I Will Survive, alongside UB40's unnecessary cover of Elvis' (I Can't Help) Falling in Love With You, shine a light on some very safe pop music being released by the record companies of the day. What the charts needed in July 1993 was for someone to come along and shake them up. Alongside Weller, five lads from Manchester were about to do just that.

Single 5:

Wild Wood
Released: 23rd August 1993; UK Chart Position: 14; Label: Go! Discs; Album: *Wild Wood*
B-sides: Ends of the Earth

UK Official Singles Chart – Top 10 – 29th August 1993:

1. Mr Vain – Culture Beat
2. It Keeps Rainin' (Tears in My Eyes) – Bitty McLean
3. The River of Dreams – Billy Joel
4. Living on my Own (1993) – Freddie Mercury
5. Right Here – SWV
6. The Key The Secret – Urban Cookie Collective
7. Nuff Vibes EP – Apache Indian
8. Higher Ground – UB40
9. Dreamlover – Mariah Carey
10. Faces – 2 Unlimited

....

14. Wild Wood – Paul Weller

Audiences have always responded incredibly well to Weller's more gentle, introspective side, despite his own embarrassment at penning slower paced songs about personal issues. Nowhere is this truer than with the decision to leave English Rose off the track listing (but not off the record itself) to *All Mod Cons* back in 1978, despite the song's immediate popularity.

As he aged though, luckily for his audience, he delved further into this side of his song writing talent, creating some of his best and most well-loved tracks. Today, his most streamed song on Spotify is You Do Something to Me (way out in front with 30 million plays), in at number 3 is Broken Stones (with 13 million), and at number 2 is the song that beat both of them into the charts, Wild Wood (with 18 million plays), his fifth solo single and the one that gave its name to his second solo album. "'Wild Wood' was my attempt at trying to write a very modern-day folk song," says Paul.[v] As Paolo Hewitt says of the song, "There is not a note out of place, nor one false move.

This is as close as you will get to some kind of perfection within the man's body of work".[vi]

In a November 2021 *Guardian* poll of Weller's best songs (from all three phases of his career), Wild Wood came in at number 4, his highest placing solo track (That's Entertainment, Going Underground and Shout to the Top! made up the top 3). Of the song they say, "The gorgeously understated music suggests getting it together in the country, but – as on Weller favourite Nick Drake's Bryter Layter – the lyrical setting is distinctly urban"[vii]. From the same poll, Sunflower, the opening track to *Wild Wood*, came in at number 11.

By the time of the single's release, Weller's position was growing stronger, and peaking at number 14, Wild Wood was his highest charting solo single to date.

Although, to look at what was in the top 10 that week, it's not a huge surprise. Mainstream dance music was still in its golden age, and Mr Vain ("Call him Mr. Raider, call him Mr. Wrong, call him insane!") by Culture Beat was at the top spot, with the bizarrely named Urban Cookie Collective's The Key The Secret at number 6, and 2 Unlimited in at number 10 with a song that wasn't No Limit.

Freddie Mercury, making the most of his posthumous career, was in at number 4 with a remix of Living on My Own (down from number 1 in July), a track which had only made it to number 50 when it was first released back in 1985, and Mariah Carey was experiencing one of her early hits with Dreamlover. Quite the eclectic mix.

Album 2:

Wild Wood
Released: 6th September 1993; UK Chart Position: 2; Label: Go! Discs
Track Listing: Sunflower; Can You Heal Us (Holy Man); Wild Wood; Instrumental (Pt 1) [Weller/Lynch/White]; All the Pictures on the Wall; Has My Fire Really Gone Out?; Country; Instrumental Two (Weller/Lynch/White); 5th Season; The Weaver; Instrumental One (Pt 2) [Weller/Lynch/White]; Foot of the Mountain; Shadow of the Sun; Holy Man (reprise); Moon on Your Pyjamas; Hung Up (featured on the 1994 release)
Producer/s: Paul Weller; Brendan Lynch

UK Official Albums Chart – Top 10 – 12th September 1993:

1. *Bat Out of Hell II – Back into Hell* – Meat Loaf
2. ***Wild Wood* – Paul Weller**
3. *Promises and Lies* – UB40
4. *Music Box* – Mariah Carey
5. *Post Historic Monsters* – Carter USM
6. *River of Dreams* – Billy Joel
7. *Pocket Full of Kryptonite* – The Spin Doctors
8. *Levellers* – Levellers
9. *Ten Summoner's Tales* – Sting
10. *Automatic for the People* – REM

Wild Wood

Although Weller had spent the eighties proving that he never followed trends or musical movements,

Wild Wood fit perfectly into the zeitgeist of the changing British musical scene in the early nineties, an environment where guitars and integrity would come to mean something again. It arrived in a sweet spot before the pomposity of the Britpop years reached their pinnacle, when an understated record could suggest the power of restraint.

Leaving behind the modern R&B of The Style Council and his debut, *Wild Wood* sees Weller rediscover the instrument that made him a success, the guitar, the aggression that made the early Jam records so exciting now transformed into an intense, philosophical introspection. The energy he lost somewhere in the eighties is back, and the record offers a depth to his bourgeoning solo career that at once mines inner turmoil, whilst simultaneously positioning himself firmly within the guitar based indie-rock camp without too closely linking his music to it. A wise move considering what was just around the corner.

Packed with strong radio-friendly songs tinged with melancholia, like the euphonic Sunflower, and the title track, the guitar licks and lyrical depth provide an accessible edge, and, although it is far from contrived, this is the album that Weller's fans wanted from him in 1993, showcasing a deepening level of musical intuition that would prove so key as his solo career matured. A judgement reflected in the album's strong chart performance, landing straight in at number 2 in a top 10 packed with rock outfits that Weller would have hated and one place behind Meat Loaf, who he would have despised.

There may be a downbeat acoustic feel to *Wild Wood*, but this isn't Weller does *MTV Unplugged*, rather, the Lennon-like piano of Can You Heal Us (Holy Man)? or the plucked acoustic of the title track in fact fit the more thoughtful approach to the developing nature of his song writing. In addition, the blue-eyed soul is far from gone, and is still very evident in the distinct and highly individual gravel of Weller's voice and in the instrumental jams, which are credited to Weller, White and Lynch, indicating that the artist is not the only driving musical force on the album.

All the Pictures on the Wall is a track of haunting beauty, matched by a contemplative lyric in which Weller asks what happens to love once death parts you ("all the pictures on the wall, serve only to remind you of it all, the wasted days we could have lived"); while Has My Fire Really Gone Out?, led by a country-style harmonica, continues the album's introspection, lyrically questioning one's relevance with age, but is augmented by a Jam style musical coda at its conclusion.

The following track Country, another heartfelt acoustic number, wouldn't have sounded out of place on a Neil Young album, and is named after the debt it owes to country music. Noel Gallagher was clearly taking notes, and the early Oasis B-sides Take Me Away is Gallagher snr. attempting to recreate the song's message about escaping from trapped circumstance with someone you love.

The second half of the record starts off with the upbeat funk of 5th Season, one of the album high points and a track that owes something of a debt to *Let it Bleed* era Rolling Stones, with Gimme Shelter-esque harmonica and screeching guitar as well as the welcome return of Dee C. Lee on backing vocals. Lyrically, the track lays bare where Weller's head is at, summing up the feel across the whole album:

A storm is raging inside my head
The wind is howling such thoughts of death
Why am I so lost and confused?
Can't find the reason for feeling blue
There's so much I can't explain
Hope this season changes soon

Third single The Weaver is classic Weller, or rather, it is the type of indie-soul-folk-rock that we will soon think of as classic Weller, and even features two of his new best friends, Simon Fowler and Steve Cradock from Ocean Colour Scene on backing vocals and guitar respectively.

Weller first stumbled across the fledgling group, whose debut album had bombed in 1992, and asked them to support him live. Noel Gallagher then saw them and asked them to support Oasis, and this seemed to give them the impetus to pen some good tunes. Their second album *Moseley Shoals* was released in April 1996 and went to number 2, and its follow up *Marchin' Already* hit the top spot a year later, and they soon became one of the most successful British groups of the Britpop era.

Cradock in particular has been with Weller for more than 20 years, playing on nearly all of his solo albums and is one of his closest musical collaborators. Although the first time they met, it very nearly didn't work out that way. As Cradock said to Ian Snowball:

I worked on 'The Weaver' before Paul had asked me to join the band...I was staying with a girlfriend who lived in London at the time and Paul phoned up saying he wanted to play me something and could I go around to his place. I was so nervous, properly shitting myself, so I swallowed a load of dope. By the time I got to Paul's front door it was really hitting me, sweaty hands and everything. Paul opened the door and I stepped inside and then I see Dee C Lee and by this point I'm tripping. I'm thinking, shit it's Paul Weller and Dee C Lee. Paul then showed me up to one of the bedrooms and he gave me a Small Faces album.[viii]

The acoustic is back out for Foot of the Mountain, another song on which he asks to be taken away, this time "on your sailboat ride". Being at the foot of the mountain suggests an awareness of the long journey ahead, so covering similar thematic ground to Shadow of the Sun, on which he asks, "Remember when we wanted to fly forever on a magic carpet ride?" The imagery of transport and being transported away runs throughout the songs on *Wild Wood*, just as the theme of nature does. The very idea of the wild wood is a clear and evocative metaphor for being lost in a harsh environment.

Unlike most Weller albums, *Wild Wood* feels like it's led by the lyrics, the music rising and swelling in support of the poetry, rather than the other way around, often sitting comfortably in the background like a Leonard Cohen or Bob Dylan album, in places reduced to just an acoustic guitar. When the music does take over, like on the long fade out to Shadow of the Sun, there is still an element of restraint, as if he is unsure whether such extended jams will gel with the audience, and so doesn't want to totally let go just yet.

Moon on Your Pyjamas is the closest to the sound of *Paul Weller*, a soul-influenced jazzy number that meanders on at a gentle pace, in no hurry to get anywhere, and completed by a partly ridiculous lyric claiming the object of the song has the "moon on your pyjamas and the stars in your eyes". It was the first track Weller penned for any of his children (he has eight to date), dedicating the song to his eldest, Nathaniel, who had just turned five.

On the original release, Moon was the final track, Hung Up, the final single, was included on the 1994 re-release of the album, because the single went to number 11 in April.

Ironically enough, *Wild Wood* is an album about insecurity, fear of rejection, and wishing for escape from a world that has spat you out, while its release brought its author back into that very world to be taken seriously as a recording artist once again. Never again would his lyrics be so personal or fragile, and the success of the album finally offered him the acceptance his career needed, confirming his place as a solo artist. It remains one of his best, and most well-loved albums.

Single 6:

The Weaver EP
Released: 1st November 1993; UK Chart Position: 18; Label: Go! Discs; Album: *Wild Wood*
B-sides: This Is No Time (Weller/Mark Alan Nelson); Another New Day (Lynch/Weller/White); Ohio (live – Royal Albert Hall, October 1992) [Ben Darlow/Neil Young)

UK Official Singles Chart – Top 10 – 7th September 1993:

1. I'd Do Anything for Love (But I Won't Do That) – Meat Loaf
2. Please Forgive Me – Bryan Adams
3. Don't Be a Stranger – Dina Carroll
4. Got to Get It – Culture Beat
5. U Got 2 Let the Music – Cappella
6. Give it Up (1993) – Goodmen
7. Hero – Mariah Carey
8. Real Love '93 – The Time Frequency
9. Feels Like Heaven – Urban Cookie Collective
10. Little Fluffy Clouds (1993) – The Orb

....

18. The Weaver EP – Paul Weller

With the top two spots of the top 10, and five in the top 20, occupied by rock acts, guitar music was once again prevalent in the charts, and Weller was a key part of that revival.

Within six months Blur would release *Parklife*, the first million selling rock album of the nineties, and guitar bands would find themselves at the centre of the zeitgeist for the first time since Weller first picked up a guitar at the end of the seventies.

Single 7:

Hung Up
Released: 28th March 1994; UK Chart Position: 11; Label: Go! Discs; Album: *Wild Wood*
B-sides: Foot of the Mountain (Live – the Royal Albert Hall, 23.11.93); The Loved; Kosmos (Lynch Mob Bonus Beats)

UK Official Singles Chart – Top 10 – 3rd April 1994:

1. Everything Changes – Take That
2. Doop – Doop
3. Streets of Philadelphia – Bruce Springsteen
4. The Most Beautiful Girl in the World – Symbol (Prince)
5. The Sign – Ace of Base
6. U R the Best Thing – D:Ream
7. I'll Remember – Madonna
8. Like to Move It – Reel 2 Real ft. Mad Stuntman
9. Without You – Mariah Carey
10. Whatta Man – Salt n Pepa with En Vogue

……………………………………

11. Hung Up – Paul Weller

Weller's seventh solo single, the Kinks-esque Hung Up, has an album bonus track feel to it, so when it appeared as a single in March 1994, reaching number 11 in the charts, it perhaps had more to do with Weller's growing reputation at this time, the eve of Britpop, than with the song itself.

That said, to look at the top 10 in April 1994, it would be easy to miss the fact that a guitar based musical movement was just around the corner. Everything Changes was the fourth number 1 single in a row from boyband Take That, as well as taking the auspicious title as the first number 1 single to feature Robbie Williams on lead vocals, and the likes of Ace of Base, Madonna (in her pre-*Ray of Light* reinvention phase) and Mariah Carey litter the charts with the type of simple pop music that Weller would surely not have appreciated.

Live Album 1:

Live Wood
Released: 9th September 1994; UK Chart Position: 13; Label: Go! Discs
Track Listing: Bull Rush/Magic Bus (Townsend)*; This is No Time*; All the Pictures on the Wall*; Remember How We Started/Dominoes**; Above the Clouds**; Wild Wood**; Shadow of the Sun^; (Can You Heal Us) Holy Man?/War (Whitfield/Strong)**; 5th Season*; Into Tomorrow^*; Foot of the Mountain*; Sunflower^; Has My Fire Really Gone Out?^
Producer: Paul Weller

*recorded live at The Royal Albert Hall, 22nd November 1993
**recorded live at Wolverhampton Civic Hall, 9th March 1994
^recorded live at Paradiso, 16th April 1994
^*recorded live at La Luna, 17th April 1994

UK Official Albums Chart – Top 10 – 18th September 1994:

1. *From the Cradle* – Eric Clapton
2. *The 3 Tenors in Concert 1994* – Carrera/Domingo /Pavarotti
3. *Definitely Maybe* – Oasis
4. *Parklife* – Blur
5. *End of Part One – Their Greatest Hits* – Wet Wet Wet
6. *Disco 2* – Pet Shop Boys
7. *Twelve Deadly Cyns... And Then Some* – Cyndi Lauper
8. *The Essential Collection* – Elvis Presley
9. *Simply the Best* – Tina Turner

10. *Music for the Jilted Generation* – Prodigy

……………………………………………

13. *Live Wood – Paul Weller*

By September, 1994 was shaping up to have a bit of something for everyone. Space for the new young guns was carved out in the shape of Oasis, Blur and the Prodigy, the old fogies would have been happy with a new album from Clapton and a new best-of from Elvis (the *Essential Collection*, the many other best-ofs being apparently inessential). And there was even room for the opera lovers, with the 3 Tenors at number 2, the trio famously kept from the top spot three weeks earlier by the debut album from Weller's best mates Oasis, which would go on to become one of the bestselling albums of the year.

Weller himself was keeping his eye in with *Live Wood*, his first live album, just missing out on the top 10. Not that he would have minded, he was just about to experience the biggest success of his entire career.

Real Success

The past was clearly on Weller's mind when he made what would become his most successful album, *Stanley Road*, in early 1995. Not only is the album named after the street where he grew up in Woking, but the cover – designed by Sir Peter Blake, who also designed *Sgt. Pepper's Lonely Hearts Club Band*, back in 1967 – is adorned with an eclectic range of key images from his past, including pictures of John Lennon, footballer George Best, the statue of Eros in Piccadilly Circus, the pre-Raphaelite painting *The Lady of Shalott* by Waterhouse, a mod scooter (of course), a green bus he used to ride in Woking, and the Eiffel Tower in Paris.

Weller also employed one of his childhood heroes, Steve Winwood from Traffic, to play Hammond Organ on Woodcutter's Son, as well as his old friend Mick Talbot, the other half of The Style Council. This, combined with the help of his semi-permanent band (including co-producer and multi-instrumentalist Brendan Lynch, keyboardist Helen Turner and drummer Steve White, the bass guitar being passed around between Dr Robert, Marco Nelson and Yolanda Charles), and new friends Steve Cradock and Noel Gallagher, meant the album managed to perfectly capture the history of Weller's specific brand of rock 'n' soul whilst maintaining something of a contemporary sound.

The first result of the new album was the album's first single, Out of the Sinking, which would late be reissued after the success of the album in March 1996. Quite why he didn't leap straight into the obviousness of The Changingman as the lead single, surely the most perfect first single off an album since In the City, is anyone's guess, but Out of the Sinking, a beautiful slice of soul flecked rock, announced to the world that Weller had some amazing songs up his sleeve.

Single 8:

Out of the Sinking
Released: 24th October 1994/26th February 1996;
UK Chart Position: 20/16; Label: Go! Discs;
Album: *Stanley Road*
B-sides: Sexy Sadie (Lennon/McCartney);
Sunflower (Lynch Mob Dub)

UK Official Singles Chart – Top 10 – 5th November 1994:

1. Baby Come Back – Pato Banton
2. Always – Bon Jovi
3. Saturday Night – Whigfield
4. Sweetness – Michelle Gayle
5. She's Got that Vibe – R Kelly
6. Welcome to Tomorrow – Snap! ft. Summer
7. Oh Baby I… – Eternal
8. Hey Now (Girls Just Wanna Have Fun) – Cyndi Lauper
9. Some Girls – Ultimate Chaos
10. Say (I Missed You) – Lisa Loeb & Nina Stories

……………………………………………………

20. Out of the Sinking – Paul Weller

With a top ten comprised mostly of early contemporary R&B – not the type of sixties R&B Weller listened to – such as (the later disgraced) R Kelly, Michelle Gayle and Eternal, it is good to see so much diversity in the charts in 1994, considering that the very white Britpop was just about to take over. However, the less sophisticated music of Whigfield and Pato Banton meant disposable pop was still very much alive and well and cluttering up the air waves.

Just 15 months later in March 1996, when Out of the Sinking was rereleased, the biggest band in Britain were Weller's mates Oasis, and their influence on the charts showed.

UK Official Singles Chart – Top 10 – 3rd March 1996:

1. How Deep is Your Love – Take That
2. Don't Look Back in Anger – Oasis
3. Children – Robert Miles
4. Coming Home Now – Boyzone

5. Going Out – Supergrass
6. Passion – Gat Decor
7. Anything – 3T
8. Good Thing – Eternal
9. I Wanna Be a Hippie – Technohead
10. I Got 5 on It – Luniz

....

16. Out of the Sinking – Paul Weller

Down from the top spot the week before, the first Oasis single to feature Noel Gallagher on lead vocals, Don't Look Back in Anger, went on to be one of their biggest. Weller first heard the song when Noel played it live acoustic and spotted it for the incredible single that he knew it would be.

He ended up lending a hand on the accompanying album, playing lead guitar on the closing track of *(What's the Story) Morning Glory?*, Champagne Supernova.

Single 9:

The Changingman
Released: 24th April 1995; UK Chart Position: 7;
Label: Go! Discs; Album: *Stanley Road*
B-sides: I'd Rather Go Blind (Billy Foster/Ellington Jordan, for Etta James); It's A New Day, Baby; I Didn't Mean to Hurt You (Live)

Weller's highest charting solo single to date was also one of his most well-known songs. Its evocative title – named after one of daughter Leah's dolls – also gave its name to Paolo Hewitt's 2007 biography of Weller. As one of his closest friends, there are few writers who have a) the kind of access to Weller that

Hewitt does, and b) has the kind of insights and understanding of him and his music, therefore it suggests that title-wise, there are few that best sum up Weller's solo career than this. The Changingman he is.

UK Official Singles Chart – Top 10 – 30th April 1995:

1. Some Might Say – Oasis
2. Back for Good – Take That
3. Key to My Life – Boyzone
4. Two Can Play That Game – Bobby Brown
5. Don't Stop (Wiggle Wiggle) – Outhere Brothers
6. Chains – Tina Arena
7. **The Changingman – Paul Weller**
8. If You Only Let Me In – MN8
9. Have You Ever Really Loved a Woman? – Bryan Adams
10. Army of Me – Bjork

With Oasis at the top spot with their first number 1, Weller appears at number 7 like a benevolent uncle, providing support for the new kids on the block and saving the world from the likes of the Outhere Brothers.

Weller would return to the top 10 many times over the coming years, but it is on this song that he hits his commercial peak, fitting considering the musical movement going on.

Album 3:

Stanley Road
Released: 15th May 1995; UK Chart Position: 1;
Label: Go! Discs

Track Listing: The Changingman (Lynch/Weller); Porcelain Gods; I Walk on Gilded Splinters (John Creaux); You Do Something to Me; Woodcutter's Son; Time Passes...; Stanley Road; Broken Stones; Out of the Sinking; Pink on White Walls; Whirlpools' End; Wings of Speed
Producer/s: Paul Weller; Brendan Lynch

UK Official Albums Chart – Top 10 – 21st May 1995:

1. ***Stanley Road* – Paul Weller**
2. *Nobody Else* – Take That
3. *I Should Coco* – Supergrass
4. *The Complete* – Stone Roses
5. *Picture This* – Wet Wet Wet
6. *The Colour of My Love* – Celine Dion
7. *Greatest Hits* – Bruce Springsteen
8. *No Need to Argue* – The Cranberries
9. *Definitely Maybe* – Oasis
10. *Medusa* – Annie Lennox

In May 1995 Weller's *Stanley Road* topped a chart filled with an impressive array of contemporary guitar music – Supergrass, The Cranberries, Oasis – whose success was all made possible thanks to the band at number 4 in the top 10 that week.

Despite their early nineties shift toward the use of drum loops and synths on classic tracks like Fools Gold, The Stone Roses' debut album had been heavily indebted to sixties guitar bands like The Small Faces and The Byrds. It had eventually shifted a million copies, the first guitar album of the era to do so, and with the back-to-back releases of two other million sellers in 1994, *Parklife* and *Definitely Maybe*, indie bands were back in fashion as 1994 turned into 1995.

A&R scouts were soon hurriedly looking around for the next big thing, and before anyone knew what was happening the charts were flooded with the likes of Supergrass, Sleeper, Menswear, Shed 7 and The Bluetones, most of whom claimed an influence from the Modfather himself.

Weller's most successful album marked the zenith of his solo career, the point where his creative and commercial capabilities met perfectly. How satisfying it must have been for an album, particularly one so autobiographical, to chime so perfectly with the tastes of the record buying public at the same time.

Stanley Road

Quietly building his solo career up over the course of two very fine albums, tonally Weller's music had been leading towards *Stanley Road* naturally. So, when guitar music suddenly became fashionable again, his timing could have not been more perfect. In April 1995, The Changingman launched its way into the top 10 and it became evident that Weller was going to be one of the key artists of the contemporary movement, his individual brand of retro-chic allying perfectly with the music of the day.

Alongside End of the Century, Some Might Say and Babies, the radio wouldn't stop playing The Changingman, and when *Stanley Road* followed as the long hot summer began, things moved at a much quicker pace for Weller than they had for a long time.

The guitar heavy sound of the album chimed so perfectly with what was in vogue in 1995 that the album shifted more copies than any Weller album to date, heading straight to number 1, quickly going x4 platinum (1.2million sales). It didn't receive universal praise though, the *NME* thinking it overly retro, damning it on its release with faint praise, by saying:

> *He [Weller] signalled his easy-noodling, pastoral rockin' intentions with last year's 'Wildwood', and 'Stanley Road' takes those ideas to conclusions that are divided almost equally by the faintly exhilarating and the harmlessly soporific"*[ix].

But despite this, the album hit the spot with its audience and Weller's imperial phase continued.

Gone is the acoustic of *Wild Wood*, exchanged for a more grown-up piano sound on tracks like the upbeat Stanley Road and the modern classic You Do Something to Me, while Broken Stones employs the (so retro its modern) Fender Rhodes (played by ex-Style Councillor, Mick Talbot). The influences are still being displayed for all to see, The Changingman's foot-stamper of a rock riff is nabbed from the Beatles' Dear Prudence, but here, as a standout track, it still claims its own distinct identity. Well, if you're gonna steal, steal from the best.

Also included is his first cover version. Walk on Gilded Splinters by Dr John is so balls-out and the confidence in Weller's performance makes it all his own, in just the same way that it is almost impossible to think Jimi Hendrix didn't write All Along the Watchtower. New mate Noel Gallagher also guests on acoustic guitar (as stated above, Weller would return the favour with a sonorous solo on Champagne Supernova), adding yet another link to the contemporary musical world onto the album. When it came to the Oasis vs. Blur chart battle just around the corner in August (the moment that Britpop crashed over into the mainstream proper), there was no doubting whose side Weller was on.

The album is as retro as the *NME* claimed, but with the hindsight of the 26 years since its release, the moniker of the "doggedly retro and straight ahead record"[x] that Ted Kessler called it in 1995, no longer needs to be taken in the negative manner with which it was initially inferred. Rather, *Stanley Road*'s retro musicality is purposefully rooted in the past as a means of expressing its themes of transformation and change, of learning from the past to create a better future. As Weller states on the opening number: "our time is on loan, only ours to borrow, but I can't be today, I can be tomorrow".

The song writer is looking forward to a brighter future, just as he had done on his first solo single, Into Tomorrow; but unlike the album's predecessor *Wild Wood*, the music aims to replicate this positive tone, which in turn makes it more accessible. *Stanley Road* is *Wild Wood* part II, but Weller has opened up his writing, fully aware of who he is aiming his material at.

Weller develops the mournful optimism of the song Wild Wood ("climbing, forever trying, finding your way out of the wild, wild wood"), but insists the music is more upbeat and more obviously tuneful than any of his previous records. The themes are the same, travelling and struggling on toward better things, like in The Changingman and Out of the Sinking: "Across the water, there's a boat that, will take us away", or about the fragility of worshiping unreal idols on Porcelain Gods ("beware false prophets... Just a porcelain god, that shatters when it falls").

Broken Stones continues the use of water and the sea to mean transience and displacement: "like pebbles on a beach, kicked around, displaced by feet". But this time Weller even refers to "a loser's reach, too slow and short to hit the peaks", inadvertently suggesting what might be an inert fear of loss, or of losing.

Like Weller's career at this point, the album has a forward momentum (the last track is even called Wings of Speed), a journey forward that is perhaps hindered by unknown or unseen obstacles, hence the continued use of water, which represents the troubled and discombobulated nature of forward motion but is constantly moving none the less.

Elsewhere, Weller's optimism isn't without its cracks. The obviousness of a ballad such as You Do Something to Me (this album's English Rose), is augmented not only by lines that challenge its message of the simple purity of love ("hoping to get close to you, a peace I cannot find"), but is later offset by Time Passes, a song about how youthful love is marred by the inevitable passing of time.

Most importantly though, the album's success confirmed Weller's traditionalist approach to song writing (lifted from Lennon/McCartney, Jagger/Richards and Steve Marriott), influencing not only Noel Gallagher and Ocean Colour Scene, but later also Pete Doherty, Luke Haines from The Kooks, and Alex Turner from Arctic Monkeys, passing on the flame that lives on to this day. The theory that the song is king, and the song writer is just the vessel for the material. Ultimately, as we'll come to see, this is Weller's chief legacy, and one to be proud of.

Stanley Road might not be the best work of Weller's career – his musical journey is too long and varied to pinpoint one specific 'best' period – but it is close to it and is certainly his most popular. It is also certain that without it, he would not have had the solo career that he has had, nor would he have had the reputation that he has today. Classics like The Changingman and You Do Something to Me, along with the huge success of *Stanley Road*, finally freed him from The Jam and The Style Council for good and set him up as a solo artist, first and foremost.

Single 10:

You Do Something to Me
Released: 10th July 1995; UK Chart Position: 9;
Label: Go! Discs; Album: *Stanley Road*
B-sides: My Whole World Is Falling Down (Crutcher/Jones/William Bell); A Year Late*; Woodcutter's Son*

*recorded live at BBC Radio One's Evening Session, May 1995

UK Official Singles Chart – Top 10 – 16th July 1995:

1. Boom Boom Boom – Outhere Brothers
2. Alright/Time – Supergrass
3. Shy Guy – Diana King
4. A Girl Life You – Edwyn Collins
5. In the Summertime – Shaggy ft. Rayvon
6. Hold Me, Thrill Me, Kiss Me, Kill Me – U2
7. Unchained Melody/White Cliffs of Dover – Robson & Jerome
8. Kiss From a Rose/I'm Alive – Seal
9. **You Do Something to Me – Paul Weller**
10. 3 is Family – Dana Dawson

Filled with Britpop classics such as Alright by Supergrass and A Girl Like You by Edwyn Collins, the

July 1995 chart was still sadly unable to save the world from the Outhere Brothers, who were at number 1 with Boom Boom Boom for its second week.

The third single from *Stanley Road*, and Weller's most streamed song on *Spotify* (31.8m plays at time of writing), You Do Something to Me, peaked at number 9 in the charts. Written less about a specific person and more about the idea of love, the tender ballad, led by its evocative ascending piano line, finds Weller at his most heartfelt. It also came in at number 22 in The Guardian's poll of best Weller tracks in November 2021, the poll calling, "a supreme bit of songwriting"[xi].

The chart in July 1995 is not just packed with Britpop favourites, it was a time for classic tracks in all genres. Two songs from the soundtrack of the third Batman film in the series begun by Tim Burton in 1989, *Batman Forever* (Schumacher, 1995) featured in the chart that week. Which, in terms of lasting reputation, are about as diametrically opposed as two tracks could possibly be. U2's oddly named Hold Me, Thrill Me, Kiss Me, Kill Me was immediately forgotten, whilst Seal's Kiss from a Rose has gained something of a legacy over the years.

Peaking at number 4 two weeks later, the track was originally released a year earlier, the first version reaching a disappointing number 20, until it was picked from near obscurity for Joel Schumacher's film and rereleased, eventually going on to worldwide recognition. Another example of the strange twist of fate that can find some songs reaching their chart potential, while others disappear without a trace.

Single 11:

Broken Stones
Released: 18th September 1995; UK Chart Position: 20; Label: Go! Discs; Album: *Stanley Road*
B-sides: Steam (Lynch/Weller)

UK Official Singles Chart – Top 10 – 24th September 1995:

1. Fairground – Simply Red
2. Boombastic – Shaggy
3. You Are Not Alone – Michael Jackson
4. Fantasy – Mariah Carey
5. Who the F**k is Alice? – Smokie ft. Roy 'Chubby' Brown
6. Stayin' Alive – N-Trance ft. Ricardo Da Force
7. I'll Be There For You – The Rembrandts
8. Runaway – Janet Jackson
9. La La La Hey Hey – Outhere Brothers
10. Somewhere Somehow – Wet Wet Wet

....

20. **Broken Stones – Paul Weller**

Perhaps Weller's most soulful track, Broken Stones sadly stalled at number 20, mostly due to it being the fourth single released from the album as well as offering only one new B-side. It remains a key song in his canon nonetheless and has only gained in momentum over the years.

Aside from Weller, also featuring in the charts in September 1995 were the likes of Cast, Menswear, Blur, The Verve, Garbage, Cardigans, Oasis, Dubstar, and D:Ream, letting us know that Britpop was in full swing.

The most notable release, aside from the incredible continuation of the Outhere Brothers presence in the charts, was the theme tune to *Friends*: The Rembrandts' I'll Be There For You, at number 7, down from a peak of number 3. The video featured the band playing live whilst the newly crowned kings and queens of evening TV acted zanily around them. The popularity of the nineties and noughties sitcom was immediate, which makes it surprising that it took them over a year to release the theme song as a single. It would dip in and out of the charts, finally ending an epic run in August 1997.

CHAPTER FOUR
The Island Years Pt. 1 – *Heavy Soul, Modern Classics* and *Heliocentric* (1996-2000)

Despite the huge success of *Stanley Road*, which had sold 1.2 million copies by mid-1996, Go! Discs folded just as Weller was beginning to think about a follow up to his most successful album to date. Founded by Andy Macdonald, an old friend and key supporter of Weller's solo career, the label came to life when Macdonald left the legendary Stiff Records, in 1983. Stiff had made a name for themselves releasing esoteric, underground records by leftfield bands, often considered too extreme for your usual indie label, including Madness (whose mega success funded much of the label's output throughout the eighties[xii]), Elvis Costello, The Pogues, and Ian Dury.

Macdonald began Go! Discs in a similar vein, signing first the ultra-left-wing politico Billy Bragg, next finding success with The Housemartins and their subsequent off-shoot, the even more successful Beautiful South, before signing Weller in 1992.

After Go! Discs was sold to Universal Music in 1996, Macdonald left the label and it soon floundered. It was common practice around this time for indie labels to find themselves bought out by the majors, in order to gain access to the mega funds needed to compete at the top table and give the majors some indie credibility.

The most famous example was Alan McGee's sale of Creation Records to Sony for £2million, just before the king of indie music stumbled upon Oasis, who benefited hugely from the extra funding that could be put into promo. But Macdonald wanted to run the label the way his own so left to start what would soon become Independiente. Weller would later follow Macdonald and release his 2002 album *Illumination* through the new label after Macdonald had hit the jackpot with Travis' 1999 album *The Man Who*, but in 1996, Weller was left slightly up the proverbial creek and with a new album to record.

Help came in the form of Island Records, a major label who started life as an indie, and managed to hang on to some indie credibility by signing the likes of Bob Marley, Roxy Music, Cat Stevens and later U2, and in 1994, Pulp.

The first single from *Heavy Soul*, Peacock Suit, had been released via Go! Discs in August 1996 just before the label folded, and had been Weller's biggest hit to date, peaking at number 5, but with a new deal Weller could record the new album, and he headed into Woolhall Studios in Bath (owned by Van Morrison) to record what would continue his run of hugely successful albums.

Peacock Suit came in at a deserved number 20 in the November 2021 Guardian poll of Weller's best songs (Jam, Style and solo).

Single 12:

Peacock Suit
Released: 5th August 1996; UK Chart Position: 5;
Label: Go! Discs; Album: *Heavy Soul*
B-sides: Eye of the Storm (Nelson/Weller/White)

UK Official Singles Chart – Top 10 – 11th August 1996:

1. Wannabe – The Spice Girls
2. Macerena – Los Del Rio
3. Freedom – Robbie Williams
4. Someday – Eternal
5. **Peacock Suit – Paul Weller**
6. Good Enough – Dodgy
7. Killing me Softly – Fugees
8. How Bizarre – OMC
9. Born Slippy – Underworld
10. The Crossroads – Bone Thugs-n-Harmony

It's a top 10 packed with pop-friendly classics such as Wannabe, the debut single by the only group who could claim to rivalry Oasis for the title of most talked about band of the nineties, The Spice Girls.

Against both the mega-hit that was the Fugees retelling of Roberta Flack's Killing Me Softly, and the dance classic that had found its place so aptly in the closing moments of the mega-hit film of the year *Trainspotting* (Boyle, 1996), Born Slippy by Underworld, it was a laudable indictment to Weller's popularity that he managed to reach number 5 with Peacock Suit in August 1996. Just don't ask who Bone Thugs-n-Harmony were...

The Heaviest of Souls

Album 4:

Heavy Soul
Released: 23rd June 1997; UK Chart Position: 2;
Label: Island

Track Listing: Heavy Soul (Pt. 1); Peacock Suit; Up in Suze's Room; Brushed (Weller/Nelson/White); Driving Nowhere; I Should Have Been There to Inspire You; Heavy Soul (Pt. 2); Friday Street; Science; Golden Sands; As You Lean Into the Light; Mermaids
Producer/s: Paul Weller; Brendan Lynch

UK Official Albums Chart – Top 10 – 29th June 1997:

1. *OK Computer* – Radiohead
2. ***Heavy Soul* – Paul Weller**
3. *Destination Anywhere* – Jon Bon Jovi
4. *Spice* – The Spice Girls
5. *Before the Rain* – Eternal
6. *Timeless* – Sarah Brightman
7. *Middle of Nowhere* – Hanson
8. *Always on my Mind – Ultimate Love Songs* – Elvis Presley
9. *The Best of* – Bob Dylan
10. *Stoosh* – Skunk Anansie

Denied the top spot on a technicality, sales of the album's special editions didn't count toward the total sales figures. *Heavy Soul* should have been Weller's second number 1 album in a row, but instead had to contend with second place to Radiohead's third album, the era-defining *OK Computer*. Whilst the likes of Spiritualized, the Charlatans, Blur and Texas all sat outside the top 10 with some of their best work, wouldn't have made much impact on Weller's ears either. However, it was great for the country to have some indie music selling so well.

Heavy Soul quickly went gold, selling 100k copies by 1st July 1997[xiii], and hung around in the top 10 for six weeks before slowly dropping down the chart, out of the top 100 by October 1997, just four months after its release. It wasn't as successful as *Stanley Road* but was clearly a hit with his existing fanbase and continued his run at the top.

The success of Weller's last two albums eventually led to Go! Discs attempting a revival, releasing a best-of from Weller's solo career, *Modern Classics*, in time for the Christmas market a year later, in December 1998. The success of the best-of led to a short-lived relaunch for the label in 1999, its back catalogue now lying with EMI, now owned by Universal.

Heavy Soul

As the name suggests, this is an album on which Weller is once again drawing from his influences in order to create his own very special brand of contemporary soul-rock, whilst telling us that the chief identifying feature of the album is the heavy guitar sound. But the title, near copied from The Beatles' 1965 game-changer *Rubber Soul*, has a double meaning, also suggesting Weller feels the weight of his own soul, just like the pun loving John Lennon's title suggests a fake soul. This is classic Weller, he is telling us who his influences are, whilst using those influences to create his own distinct message at the same time.

Despite its individuality, *Heavy Soul* is positioned in clear linear order behind *Wild Wood* and *Stanley Road* to finish off Weller's trilogy of nineties albums, just like both Blur and Oasis did during the Britpop period[xiv]. Like *Wild Wood* and *Stanley Road*, the songs on *Heavy Soul* range from the beautifully crafted, such as the gentle understated piano-led soul of I Should Have Been There to Inspire You, to the folky acoustic shuffle of Up in Suze's Room, but it is the four-to-the-floor rock 'n' roll of singles Peacock Suit and Brushed that dominates. Although the album also finds space for some *Abbey Road* style experimentation, such as Weller and Steve Cradock's duelling guitars on the opening title track.

Otherwise, studio experimentation is kept to a minimum. Violins fade in and out as animal noises cross from speaker to speaker on the reprise of the title track, but once again, Weller is keen to place the songs front and centre and let them speak for themselves. Thematically, the song has something very simple to say about the simple joys of life. Driving Nowhere is a mid-tempo ode to the restlessness of youth (and name sake to the Oasis track Going Nowhere, released four months later as the B-side to Stand By Me), whilst Up in Susie's Room is a romantic ballad about discovering the pleasures of first love ("warm air blows, down upon her soft bed, she licks my face and the feeling spreads").

Apart from that, the piano and the Rhodes are mostly left off the album, in favour of Weller's overdriven Epiphone and Cradock's Les Paul. Single Friday Street could have had a summer breeze feel to it if done differently, but as it is, the track has an intense distorted drone that fits into the overall guitar driven approach to the album.

Keeping things simple, the core band consists of just Weller, Cradock, Steve White and Marco Nelson on bass, with a handful of others (including Jules Holland) guesting. This means the album is more focused than any of Weller's to date, guitar, bass and drums locking together as tightly as the power trio Weller once headed up as a teenager and allowing the message of the songs to filter through unabated.

If there was much of a message to impart. Lyrically, the summery feel to the album seems to return Weller to adolescence (Up in Suze's Room, Golden Sands, Mermaids), sharing feelings about first love, or aimless drifting (Driving Nowhere). The final track, and fourth and final single, Mermaids, brings the album to a gentle conclusion. The guitars are as prominent as ever, but there is a spaced-out lazy feeling which positions the track as something of a gentle summer sing-along, particularly the 'sha-la-la' chorus. The song returns to the theme of youthful love for a free-spirited girl, reminding of long days when all you had to worry about was trying to get the girl ("she's in my head, she's in my mind").

After the intense introspection of *Wild Wood*, and the wishful dreaming of *Stanley Road*, the return to such simple pleasures, set against a guitar heavy musical backdrop, is something of a welcome relief and the album feels like the full stop on one period of Weller's career. His most commercially successful as it would turn out, but not necessarily his most important. It is easy to see though why the album, followed by a best-of, felt like the end of something. Critics mistook it for the winding down of his solo career, where history and hindsight have proven that in fact, he was just getting going and was simply freeing himself from his heavy soul.

Single 13:

Brushed*
Released: 28th July 1997; UK Chart Position: 14;
Label: Island; Album: *Heavy Soul*
B-sides: Shoot the Dove

*music by, Weller/White/Nelson; lyrics by Weller

UK Official Singles Chart – Top 10 – 3rd August 1997:

1. I'll Be Missing You – Puff Daddy ft. Faith Evans
2. Freed From Desire – Gala
3. All About Us – Peter Andre
4. Everybody (Backstreet's Back) – The Backstreet Boys
5. Black Eyed Boy – Texas
6. Mo Money Mo Problems – Notorious B.I.G.
7. Picture of You – Boyzone
8. Bitch – Meredith Brooks
9. C U When You Get There – Coolio ft. 40 Thevz
10. D'You Know What I Mean? – Oasis

……………………………………

14. Brushed – Paul Weller

Although guitar rock was still very prevalent in the charts in summer 1997, in the form of the all-conquering Oasis with one of the year's biggest singles, D'You Know What I Mean, which sold 400,000 copies on its first day of release alone[xv], Weller and the other guitar bands were also lending their influence to straight pop acts. The likes of Texas and Meredith Brooks were leaping into the top 10 by strumming guitars and penning indie-flecked pop songs.

It was another genre of music that was grabbing most of the headlines that Oasis didn't occupy in August 1997. The murder of American rapper Notorious B.I.G. in March, at the supposed hands of rival rappers (the infamous East Coast vs. West Coast war that also saw the loss of incendiary rival Tupac Shakur in September 1996) saw not only Biggie's posthumously released single, the aptly named Mo Money Mo Problems, reach number 6, but also the tribute to the rapper led by his colleague and loyal friend Puff Daddy, and his widow, Faith Evans. The huge single I'll Be Missing You was at number 1 for three weeks, before being knocked off by Oasis, before returning to number 1, for a subsequent three weeks. The single would remain in the charts for the rest of 1997 and would be seen as recently as 2009.

Single 14:

Friday Street (A *Heavy Soul* EP)
Released: 29th September 1997; UK Chart Position: 21; Label: Island; Album: *Heavy Soul*
B-sides: Sunflower (live)*; Brushed (live)*^; Mermaids (live)*

*recorded live at The Southbank
^music by, Weller/White/Nelson; lyrics by Weller

UK Official Singles Chart – Top 10 – 5th October 1997:

1. Candle in the Wind '97/Something About the Way Your Looked Tonight – Elton John
2. Sunchyme – Dario G
3. As Long As You Love Me – Backstreet Boys
4. Angel of Mine – Eternal
5. Stand by Me – Oasis
6. Raincloud – Lighthouse Family
7. Tubthumping – Chumbawamba
8. Men in Black – Will Smith
9. Got 'til It's Gone – Janet ft. Q Tip and Joni Mitchell
10. Arms Around the World – Louise

....

21. Friday Street – Paul Weller

The chief reason that D'You Know What I Mean wasn't the biggest selling single of the year, was because the release of Elton John's September 1997 single Candle in the Wind became the biggest selling single of all time, going x9 platinum, selling more than 5.4million copies[xvi] in the UK alone. The accidental death of Diana, Princess of Wales, in Paris on 31st August had been nothing less than a national tragedy that touched every soul in the country in some way, and Elton rewrote the lyrics to his 1973 single dedicated originally to Marilyn Monroe, changing "goodbye Norma Jean," to, "goodbye England's Rose", playing the song live in Westminster Abbey at her funeral.

The mood of the nation seemed to change overnight, with the years of Britpop excess meeting their swift end. The party was finally over and something as trivial as pop music suddenly didn't seem as important. With the end of 1997 came a run of hugely successful, much darker records that harnessed this change in mood, shifting it toward a darker, moodier style. The likes of Spiritualized, Radiohead and The Verve all found much success in later 1997 with a sound that was at odds with Weller's music.

Single 15:

Mermaids
Released: 24th November 1997; UK Chart Position: 30; Label: Island; Album: *Heavy Soul*
B-sides: So You Want to be a Dancer (Weller/Lynch/Nelson/Matt Deighton/White); Everyone Has a Price to Pay

UK Official Singles Chart – Top 10 – 30th November 1997:

1. Perfect Day – Various Artists
2. Baby Can I Hold You/Shooting Star – Boyzone
3. Barbie Girl – Aqua
4. Wind Beneath My Wings – Steven Houghton
5. Torn – Natalie Imbruglia
6. Never Ever – All Saints
7. Lucky Man – The Verve
8. Tell Him – Barbara Streisand and Celine Dion
9. Ain't That Just the Way – Lutricia McNeal
10. Candle in the Wind '97/Something About the Way You Looked Tonight – Elton John

....

30. Mermaids – Paul Weller

As it was the last single from the album and offered nothing particularly new to fans that they hadn't already heard on *Heavy Soul*, there was little surprise that the end-of-summer jangle Mermaids only just dented the top 30.

Originally released on 22nd November 1997, Never Ever by All Saints would achieve what singles almost never did in the nineties, namely find their way to number 1 after being on the chart for a number of weeks, in this instance a nearly unprecedented nine weeks later.

Back in the sixties it was common for singles to make their way slowly up the chart over the course of a few weeks, but with marketing prior to a release reaching near saturation point in the mid-nineties, most singles peaked at their highest place in their first week. Never Ever went twice platinum at the end of January 1998, having first gone platinum on

5th December 1997, meaning it sold 600k copies in six weeks.

Therefore, when it reached the top spot on 17th January 1998, it was likely one of the lowest selling number 1 singles of the decade, selling just 100k copies to reach the top of the charts[xvii]. This is compared to the 270,000 copies that Blur's Country House sold in August 1995, just three years earlier[xviii]. The singles chart it seemed, was in trouble.

Single 16:

Brand New Start
Released: 26th October 1998; UK Chart Position: 16; Label: Island; Album: *Modern Classics – The Greatest Hits*
B-sides: Right Underneath It; The Riverbank

UK Official Singles Chart – Top 10 – 8th November 1998:

1. Believe – Cher
2. Each Time – E-17
3. If You Buy This Record Your Life Will Be – Tamperer ft. Maya
4. Would You? – Touch and Go
5. Another One Bites the Dust – Queen ft. Wyclef Jean, Pras and Free
6. Daydreamin' – Tatyana ft. Will Smith
7. Outside – George Michael
8. Falling in Love Again – Eagle-Eye Cherry
9. I Don't Want to Miss a Thing – Aerosmith
10. Sweetest Thing – U2

....

16. Brand New Start – Paul Weller

Released almost exactly a year after Mermaids, the deeply introspective, morning-after-the-night-before lament Brand New Start was put out to help promote the best of, *Modern Classics – The Greatest Hits*. The album drew together all of the singles from Weller's solo albums to date, both the Go! Discs years and the Island era so far.

With these singles altogether in one place for the first time, fans old and new were offered a glimpse into what was shaping up to be quite an incredible solo career. One that, dare we say it, outpaced the two previous incarnations of Weller's musical life.

Best of Album no. 1:

Modern Classics – The Greatest Hits
Released: 15th December 1998; UK Chart Position: 7; Label: Go! Discs
Track Listing: Out of the Sinking; Peacock Suit; Sunflower; The Weaver; Wild Wood; Above the Clouds; Uh Huh Oh Yeh; Brushed (Weller/White/Nelson/Lynch); The Changingman (Weller/Lynch); Friday Street; You Do Something To Me; Brand New Start; Hung Up; Mermaids; Broken Stones; Into Tomorrow
Producer/s: Paul Weller; Brendan Lynch

UK Official Albums Chart – Top 10 – 15th November 1998:

1. *Ladies & Gentlemen – The Best Of* – George Michael
2. *The Best of 1980-1990 & B-sides* – U2
3. *The Masterplan* – Oasis
4. *The Best Of* – M People
5. *Talk on Corners* – The Corrs

6. *I've Been Expecting You* – Robbie Williams
7. ***Modern Classics – The Greatest Hits* – Paul Weller**
8. *The Best of 1980-1990* – U2
9. *One Night Only* – The Beegees
10. *Supposed Former Infatuation Junkie* – Alanis Morrissette

With just three albums of original music making up the top 10 albums in November 1998, the state of the British recording industry was laid bare for all to see. The other seven albums were all best ofs, with the same album by U2 appearing twice, once with the B-sides included, once without. And Weller was no different. Not that it was his decision to release the collection and Go! Discs, without founding member Andy Macdonald, put out the record in order to gain some much needed revenue. And it worked. Although it only peaked at number 7, the album would go platinum by the end of the year, shifting more than 300k copies, proving Weller's ongoing popularity and the success of his solo work. It also proved a popular album throughout the next decade and a half, eventually going twice platinum in 2013, another nod to Weller's ongoing popularity well into the fifth decade of his recording career.

Single 17:

Wild Wood (rerelease)
Released: 28th December 1998; UK Chart Position: 22; Label: Island; Album: *Modern Classics – The Greatest Hits*
B-sides: Wild Wood (The Sheared Wood Remix); Science (A Lynch Mob Remix)

UK Official Singles Chart – Top 10 – 3rd January 1999:

1. Heartbeat/Tragedy – Steps
2. Goodbye – Spice Girls
3. Chocolate Salty Balls (p.s. I Love You) – Chef
4. Believe – Cher
5. To You I Belong – B*Witched
6. When You're Gone – Bryan Adams ft. Melanie C.
7. Especially For You – Denise and Johnny
8. Miami – Will Smith
9. End of the Line – Honeyz
10. 1999 – Prince

....

22. Wild Wood – Paul Weller

The last single released to help promote the best-of was also the rerelease of one of Weller's most loved songs: Wild Wood which, five years after its initial release, had garnered something of a legendary status amongst Weller fans. It was also his last release not only of the twentieth century, but for the next 16 months.

As unsentimental as ever, if there were any acts that had plans to release singles around the dawning of the new millennium, Weller certainly wasn't one of them, and it would be May 2000 before we saw another single from the Modfather. He's a Keeper would be the first single released from his next album *Heliocentric*, and it would do the most amazing of things, it would fail to chart, helping stir those rumours that this would be Weller's last album.

That Difficult Fifth Album

After completing several large tours and racking up hundreds of gig dates between 1995 and 1998,

Weller played live only a handful of times in 1999 and didn't appear anywhere between June 1999 and April 2000. With the benefit of hindsight, it of course looks ridiculous that he might be retiring his solo career, but just as the internet was starting to take hold of the world, those pesky chat rooms were buzzing with rumours, in just the way that stories of secret acts playing clandestine slots spread at summer festivals. "Have you heard Paul McCartney and Ringo Starr are playing the Dance tent at Reading...?" Weller just needed some time off, and by May 2000 he was back with his fifth studio album, *Heliocentric*, which for some reason was released nearly a month before the single that was supposed to promote it.

Album 5:

Heliocentric
Released: 10th April 2000; UK Chart Position: 2; Label: Island
Track Listing: He's the Keeper; Frightened; Sweet Pea, My Sweet Pea; A Whale's Tale; Back in the Fire; Dust and Rocks; There's No Drinking, After You're Dead; With Time & Temperance; Picking Up Sticks; Love-Less
Producer/s: Paul Weller; Brendan Lynch

UK Official Albums Chart – Top 10 – 16th April 2000:

1. *Play* – Moby
2. ***Heliocentric* – Paul Weller**
3. *Things to Make and Do* – Moloko
4. *Supernatural* – Santana

5. *Reload* – Tom Jones
6. *Westlife* – Westlife
7. *Northern Star* – Melanie C
8. *At His Very Best* – Engelbert Humperdinck
9. *The Man Who* – Travis
10. *Come on Over* – Shania Twain

Being kept from the top spot by Moby's multi-platinum *Play* said less about Weller than it did about the phase that British pop music was going through at the turn of the new century. Already on release for 25 weeks in April 2000, five of them at number 1, *Play* would be the fifth biggest selling album of 2000[xix], and would remain in the charts on and off for the next five years, finally dropping out in July 2005. Its key legacy was in popularising the one man alone with a sampler and keyboard movement, which Norman Cook, aka Fatboy Slim (and ex-Housemartin's bassist), had a major hand in kickstarting a few years earlier. DJs had of course been creating their own brand of dance-friendly music for decades by this point, but Slim and Moby crossed over into the mainstream properly.

Aside from Moby, Robbie Williams' brand of inoffensive man-boy pop was the biggest thing in the country. Having been launched into the big time by ripping off Oasis (Angels, Strong, Old Before I Die), he had subsequently chosen to follow the growing trend for drum loops, synths and disco choruses. His August 2000 album *Sing When Your Winning* would typify this new approach, led as it was by the massive number 1 single Rock DJ, but it would seem that Williams was only just getting going in 2000, and his fifth studio album *Escapology* would be the biggest selling album of the year in 2002, making him the first undoubted mega-star of the new millennium.

With the Britpop years in the distant past, 2000 seemed to be about new approaches to music, but pop was in fact still steeped in the retrospection of its own history. Moloko's third album *Things to Make and Do* sat just behind *Heliocentric* and was released on the same day, and it succeeded where the band's first two album had failed because it married together the best bits of disco and acid house, exemplified by the mega-hit Sing it Back, reproducing an age-old sound but with a new sheen. Not unlike what Mr Weller himself was doing.

Aside from *Heliocentric*, Travis were the only indie-rock act in the top 10, with their second album *The Man Who* signalling a place for mournful reflective music about losing out in love and life, played on an acoustic guitar. Enter another of the era's biggest acts, Coldplay.

Heliocentric

So, the times they were a-changing. However, as the old adage goes: the more things change, the more they stay the same, and if nothing else, *Heliocentric* taught us that Weller was fast becoming the constant that all the change could be measured against.

Heliocentric is far from the disaster that many painted it at the time. The Guardian damned with faint praise by saying, "If 97's ponderous *Heavy Soul* was Weller's solo nadir, *Heliocentric* is a mustering of forces"[xx]. The worst criticism that could be labelled its way is that it is Weller by numbers yet seeing as he had spent the last half a decade proving he was one of the country's best songwriters, this is no small feat. First single He's the Keeper gets things under way in classic style, a suitable tup-thumper that churns along at a mid-tempo pace, a not too distant cousin of the likes of Brushed from *Heavy Soul*, although never quite catching fire like that song does.

Second track Frightened is a piano led ballad that wouldn't have been out of place on his solo debut, complete with haunting strings, whilst track 3 and second single Sweet Pea, My Sweet Pea is an acoustic strum and gentle ode to love: "You're the girl to get my heart start jumpin' again", and probably the most listenable song on the album.

The album was recorded around the time that Weller had finally left London and moved out to the suburbs in leafy Surrey. His family life seemingly secure for the first time in his adult life, it is perhaps the lack of gritty material that means the album lacks any real edge. It's not unlike most of the Wings records from the seventies, when Weller's hero McCartney was coasting through his thirties rich and comfortable with a growing family of his own. For any other artist this might not have been an issue, but Weller had made his name by singing about the youth explosion, and explosions of any kind were very far away indeed from rural Surrey.

With a band once again stripped back to the core of Brendan Lynch, Steve White and Steve Cradock, along with Cradock's bass playing colleague in Ocean Colour Scene, Damon Minchella, the back-to-basics approach fits aptly into Weller's overall canon nicely, and it is easy to see the band enjoying themselves over a few beers and a BBQ whilst playing along to the gentle pace of Back in the Fire, A Whale's Tale and Dust and Rocks, three tracks that seem to play into each other without a break in tempo or chord structure. But this music sits somewhat awkwardly in the company of the big acts of the day: Blink 182, Basement Jaxx, Dr Dre, Steps and Britney Spears.

If there is a message to the album it is probably summed up quite nicely in track 7, There is No Drinking, After You're Dead. Sober today for more than ten years, Weller was always known to be a bit of a boozer, but this isn't a track about the perils of drinking, rather it is an old fashioned moral aimed at telling us to seize the day, to carpe diem, because "there is no love making, after your dead". It's the precursor to the next track, another that reminds of the early days of Weller's solo days, With Time and Temperance, another song on the album that interestingly also references sobriety, but is again an ode to not missing out, and being able to consider what has passed from a place of distance and time.

The album ends with Love-Less, a ballad that starts with yet another heart-felt piano line and lyrical lament that shows off Weller's gravelly voice (surely entering its best phase around this time) and giving way to the strongest chorus section on the album, led by Minchella's funky bass, and the strings that seem both strange and perfectly apt at the same time. Perhaps because they would have been so out of place at the back garden around the BBQ.

Heliocentric may have been something of a let-down to fans so enamoured by the trilogy of *Wild Wood*, *Stanley Road* and *Heavy Soul*, but it was far from being a bad album, and putting it out helped him do what he does best, namely get back out on the road.

Single 18:

He's a Keeper
Released: 1st May 2000; UK Chart Position: n/a;
Label: Island; Album: *Heliocentric*
B-sides: Heliocentric (Weller/White); Bang-Bang (Sonny Bono)

UK Official Singles Chart – Top 10 – 7th May 2000:

1. Oops! I did it Again – Britney Spears
2. Bound 4 Da Reload (Casualty) – Oxide and Neutrino
3. Heart of Asia – Watergate
4. Toca's Miracle – Coco vs. Fragma
5. The Bad Touch – Bloodhound Gang
6. Thong Song – Sisqo
7. Fill Me In – Craig David
8. Achilles Heel – Toploader
9. He Wasn't Man Enough – Toni Braxton
10. Flowers – Sweet Female Attitude

....

– **He's a Keeper – Paul Weller**

One of the worst top 10's in the history of popular music? Perhaps. But May 2000 saw Weller's latest single fail to chart, the first time this has happened in his long career. Although, would he have wanted to be included?

The short-lived UK Garage scene was on the verge of gripping the nation. Here represented by Craig David's first solo single Fill Me In, down from the top spot, and Oxide and Neutrino's odd remix of the *Casualty* theme tune. David had made his name with the first proper garage hit single, Re-Rewind (The

Crowd Say Bo Selecta) by the Artful Dodger in December 1999, and the scene would peak with its anthem 21 Seconds to Go by the So Solid Crew, which would reach number 1 in August 2001. The track would spawn the brief careers of its various members, including Romeo, Harvey, Asher D (MC turned actor Ashley Waters from *Top Boy* [2001-present]) and Lisa Mafia. As fate would have it, So Solid Crew would be signed to Independiente, Andy Macdonald's label who would also sign Weller in 2001.

The UK garage scene is so brilliantly sent up in the BBC TV series *People Just Do Nothing* (2014-present), which follows the misadventures of Kurupt FM, a pirate radio station which plays exclusively UK garage. The show uses the short lived nature of the scene, famous for moving from the credibility of the underground club scene only to lose any such credibility once it entered the pop mainstream, to expose how its cast of misfits are trapped in a moment in time, unable to grow up or escape, railing under the misapprehension that they are both current and incredibly popular. ("Get Out the way!")

In 2021 the gang returned with the first Kurupt FM feature film, which sees the them experience something of a career renaissance in… where else… that's right, Spinal Tap's final stamping ground, Japan. *People Just Do Nothing: Big in Japan* (Clough, 2021), was released in August.

So, Weller was probably best off out of it. The chief reason that the single didn't chart was most probably because it was released after the album that it was supposed to promote, and seeing as Weller's audience are classic album buyers, there was little reason to also buy the single. Shame, because everyone missed out on his great cover of Cher's Bang-Bang.

Single 19:

Sweet Pea, My Sweet Pea
Released: 21st August 2000; UK Chart Position: 44; Label: Island; Album: *Heliocentric*
B-sides: Back in the Fire (BBC Radio 2 Session); There's No Drinking, After You're Dead (Noonday Underground Remix)

UK Official Singles Chart – Top 10 – 27th August 2000:

1. Music – Madonna
2. Groovejet (If this Ain't Love) – Spiller
3. Out of Your Mind – True Steppers ft. Dane Bowers and Victoria Beckham
4. Rock DJ – Robbie Williams
5. I Turn to You – Melanie C
6. Lucky – Britney Spears
7. Freestyler – Bomfunk MC's
8. 7 Days – Craig David
9. Time to Burn – Storm
10. Doesn't Really Matter – Janet Jackson

…………………………………………………………………

44. Sweet Pea, My Sweet Pea – Paul Weller

With not one but two former Spice Girls present, Madonna back at the top spot with her tenth number 1, and Janet Jackson rounding out the top 10, it was great to see some female artists leading the charge in August 2000, as Weller's nineteenth solo single just missed out on the top 40.

Having not long split, each of the Spice Girls was launching a solo career with differing levels of success. Geri Halliwell, who left the band in 1998, had already notched up three number 1 singles; Melanie C was in second place with two number 1s, including a duet with Lisa 'Left Eye' Lopez from TLC; Mel B had taken I Want you Back with Missy Elliot to the top spot back in September 1998; and Emma Bunton would be awarded her first and only solo number 1 a year later in April 2001.

Victoria Beckham, however, would have to contend with a number 2 in August 2000. Featuring on the UK garage track alongside Dane Bowers from boy band Another Level, Out of Your Mind by True Steppers, the track was beaten to the top spot by Spiller's Groovejet (If This Ain't Love), which featured a young Sophie Ellis-Bexter. Not that Victoria was that fussed, being on the verge of becoming one of the most famous women in the world.

CHAPTER FIVE
Independiente – *Days of Speed*, *Illumination* and *Fly on The Wall: B Sides & Rarities* (2001-2003)

Weller signed to Andy Macdonald's Independiente in 2001. As previously mentioned, the label was flush from the huge success of Travis' second album *The Man Who* and would also soon experience something similar with another late Britpop outfit (and Chris Martin's best mates), Embrace, with their 2004 album, *Out of Nothing*.

Weller's first album through his new label would also be his second live album, *Days of Speed*, which hit the record store shelves in October 2001, and came about after the massive success of his biggest tour to date. Both tour and album took their name from the lyric in the Jam song, That's Entertainment, "Days of speed and slow time Mondays".

Although Weller found time to play on both a tribute album to The Who called (what else) *Substitute: Songs of the Who* and to play live with Noel Gallagher at a tribute concert for Stephen Marriott at the Astoria, the *Days of Speed* tour took up a large chunk of 2001. Weller played all over the UK as well as dates around Europe, with the tour notably different from previous outings because alongside his solo material, he also reintroduced Jam songs, and most importantly, the performances consisted of just Weller and his guitar.

The incredible reaction to the stripped back selection of songs from across Weller's career, gave him and the label cause to release it as an album, and

Days of Speed was an immediate hit, going platinum and peaking at number 3 in the charts.

Live Album 2:

Days of Speed
Released: 8th October 2001; UK Chart Position: 3; Label: Independiente
Track Listing: Brand New Start; The Loved; Out of the Sinking; Clues; English Rose; Above the Clouds; You Do Something to Me; Amongst Butterflies; Science; Back in the Fire; Down the Seine; That's Entertainment; Love-Less; There's No Drinking, After You're Dead; Everything Has a Price to Pay; Wild Wood; Headstart for Happiness; Town Called Malice; The Butterfly Collector; Carnation
Producer/s: Tony Cousins; Andrew Jones; Charles Rees

n.b. all tracks were recorded live in Berlin, London, Dublin, Rimini and Southampton, 2001

UK Official Albums Chart – Top 10 – 14th October 2001:

1. *Fever* – Kylie Minogue
2. *Love is Here* – Starsailor
3. ***Days of Speed* – Paul Weller**
4. *Songs from the West Coast* – Elton John
5. *Then and Now* – David Cassidy
6. *Collection* – Tracy Chapman
7. *The Invisible Band* – Travis
8. *No Angel* – Dido

9. *The Album* – Bob the Builder
10. *Hybrid Theory* – Linkin Park

With 9/11 just a month earlier, pop music in October 2001 was split into two definitive camps. The first was the escapist pop exemplified by Kylie's return to form album *Fever*. The album, which included the mega-hit single Can't Get You Out of My Head, remained in the charts until well into 2003 (appearing as recently as October 2021).

The other camp was typified by the dark introspection of acts like Starsailor (named after the Tim Buckley album) and their debut album *Love is Here*, which interestingly also featured a song called Fever; plus Weller's label mates Travis and their third album *The Invisible Band*; Weller himself, with his acoustic album; and *No Angel* by Dido, which was chiefly heartache sung to music and which would be the biggest selling album of the year; and even the grizzly darkness of nu-metal band Linkin Park and their massive debut *Hybrid Theory*.

The biggest event of the new millennium though would have a major impact on the type of music that people created and listened to. In just the way that the death of Princess Diana ended the Britpop party back in 1997, 9/11 would finally bring an end to the years of opulence the West had unwittingly enjoyed. The party was over. What would the world do next?

Days of Speed

Part live album, part career greatest hits album, *Days of Speed* was the perfect opportunity for Weller to reinvent himself once more, reimagining some of his most famous compositions in a new style. By stripping back the songs to their simplest parts on classics like Out of the Sinking, Above the Clouds and Town Called Malice, tracks that had always benefited from a backing band, Weller was able to open himself up to a rawer level of inspection than ever before.

By reducing them to their most basic presentation, fans were invited in to see how beautiful his songs were, plus quite how charming his voice was when set against such stark backing. The album worked at managing to add another level of dynamism to his career, without him having to come up with any new material. So important after the laissez faire reaction to *Heliocentric*.

The album's success also opened up future opportunities further down the line, including the 2003 B-sides and rarities album, *Fly on the Wall*, and the 2004 covers album, *Studio 150*. Fans now trusted Weller as a brand and would happily lap up whatever new approach to creating his music he decided to take.

Days of Speed nicely mixes together those songs that were intended for the acoustic: That's Entertainment (minus Bruce Foxton's "tra la la la laaas"), Wild Wood and English Rose, and sets them amongst a wide selection of songs usually played with the full band, You Do Something to Me, The Butterfly Collector and Carnation, providing some of the high points. It is not an easy feat to strip away the many layers to a track that were so carefully constructed in the studio, and there is always the possibility of fans rejecting the new approach, but the album positions Weller as a performer and songwriter first, and studio technician second.

It played a major part in helping maintain the level of success that he had carved out for himself by this point, and gave him the imputes to once again put pen to paper and return to the studio to record his next album of new material.

The Lights are Back On

Having spent the latter half of 2001 writing and recording *Illumination* at Noel Gallagher's Wheeler End Studio, as well as continuing with his new found love of touring, it was May 2002 before Weller released any new music, this time in the form of an appearance on the single Brother to Brother by the American soul legend Terry Callier. The blues track was taken from Callier's 2002 album *Speak Your Peace* and reached number 81 in the UK singles chart in May 2002.

Then, on 28th July, Weller continued his passion for playing live, by headlining a massive outdoor concert in Hyde Park to 50,000 eager fans. The concert would later be released on DVD as *Live in Hyde Park*, three of the tracks making it onto CD2 of the second single from *Illumination*, Leafy Mysterious.

And then it was finally time for some new music, and a welcome return to the top 10 for Weller's new single It's Written in the Stars, his highest chart entry since Peacock Suit back in August 1996. Reinvigorated by the success of *Days of Speed*, Weller embraced a new style for the first time in a long time, working with DJ Simon Dine and his band the Noonday Underground, who also co-produced the album. It was the start of a long relationship with Dine, that would see the two artists working together for Weller's next five studio albums.

Relegating his trusty Epiphone to a supporting role, It's Written in the Stars is led by a stomping looped brass refrain which sounds like it's been lifted directly from a northern soul track from the seventies, but was actually composed specially by Dine. The riff was considered so key to the song's success that Dine was even given a co-writing credit for the music.

It's Written in the Stars is about a catchy a single as Weller had released for some years, and it set the tone for the album that was to follow. There were whispers that the Modfather was back.

Single 20:

It's Written in the Stars
Released: 2nd September 2002; UK Chart Position: 7; Label: Independiente; Album: *Illumination*
B-sides: CD1: Horseshoe Drama (music: Weller/Dine; Lyrics: Weller); Push Button Automatic (music: Weller; lyrics: White)
CD2: The Butterfly Collector*; Carnation**

*recorded live at the Shepherds Bush Empire, London, 2nd June 2001
**recorded live at the Paradiso, Amsterdam, 7th February 2001

UK Official Singles Chart – Top 10 – 8th September 2002:

1. The Tide is High (Get the Feeling) – Atomic Kitten
2. Fantasy – Appleton
3. Round Round – Sugababes
4. Crossroads – Blazin' Squad
5. Addictive – Truth Hurts ft. Rakim
6. Forever – N-Trance
7. **It's Written in the Stars – Paul Weller**

8. Colourblind – Darius
9. What You Got – Abs
10. Dy-na-mi-tee – Ms Dynamite

It's slightly odd seeing Weller's name amidst the unlikely company of boybands, girl bands and solo artists that used to be in boybands and girl bands and, in the case of Darius, those that came third in *Pop Idol*, but there he was, hitting number 7 in September 2002 with his twentieth solo single in eight years.

Peaking at just 25, the White Stripes are the only clue to the new music that was making something of a stir in the indie scene at the time. Garage rock was experiencing something of a revival, led by Detroit's White Stripes and New York's The Strokes, and the scene would soon cross over into Britain to be led by The Libertines, and would play a major hand in kickstarting a second wave of Britpop bands flooding the charts in 2003. The likes of Keane, Snow Patrol, Hard Fi, Razorlight, Elbow, Doves, Badly Drawn Boy, The Pigeon Detectives, The Coral and The Zutons, would all find themselves doing incredibly well in the coming years. Citing Oasis, Blur, and of course, Weller, as key influences.

Album 6:

Illumination
Released: 16th September 2002; UK Chart Position: 1; Label: Independiente
Track Listing: Going Places; A Bullet for Everyone; Leafy Mysteries; It's Written in the Stars; Who Brings Joy; Now the Night is Here (Weller/Dine); Spring (At Last); One X One; Bag Man; All Good

Books; Call Me No.5 (Weller/Kelly Jones); Standing Out in the Universe; Illumination
Producer/s: Paul Weller; Simon Dine

UK Official Albums Chart – Top 10 – 22nd September 2002:

1. ***Illumination* – Paul Weller**
2. *A Rush of Blood to the Head* – Coldplay
3. *Feels So Good* – Atomic Kitten
4. *Missundaztood* – Pink
5. *Nellyville* – Nelly
6. *Imagine* – Eva Cassidy
7. *Escape* – Enrique Iglesias
8. *The Eminem Show* – Eminem
9. *Heathen Chemistry* – Oasis
10. *A Little Deeper* – Ms Dynamite

Looking at the top 10 in October 2002, you could be forgiven for thinking it was 1997 again, with guitar bands fighting it out with rap acts amongst a safe haven of a handful of pop outfits. Thanks predominantly to the mega success of Coldplay, whose second album *A Rush of Blood to the Head* had just been released, going straight to number 1 and hanging around for well over a year in the charts, guitar music was back. Oasis too were experiencing something of a rebirth, that coincided nicely with Weller's return to form, and *Heathen Chemistry*, their first with their new line up, would be their biggest of the new millennium.

Illumination

Recorded at Noel Gallagher's Wheeler End Studios in the latter half of 2001, Gallagher also played on several tracks on the album, notably adding sparse drums to One X One, a mostly acoustic number reminiscent of Wild Wood. Gallagher, not noted for his drum playing, commented that Weller's approach to recording was often as egalitarian as it could be restrictive. He said, "The point is, it doesn't matter who or what you are, or even if you play something that is technically wrong or just sounding shit, if it feels right to Paul, it stays"[xxi], adding that he had just as often found his guitar playing ditched on the final record without pre-warning.

Gallagher, who had played on several of his best mate's albums over the years, also commented that the loose recording of the album was, "done at a strange time; the last record he made of that ilk"[xxii]. Quite why this record is singled out as the last of anything is unclear, other than perhaps to suggest that the looseness of Weller's recording would be finished with after *Illumination*, and a seriousness would enter into the studio that saw him always rejecting the first take, even if it was perfect, instead insisting on however many takes were required to satisfy his arbitrary process.

Similar to *Heliocentric*, there is a kind of summery looseness to *Illumination*, which was also Weller's first solo effort not to feature Brendan Lynch at the mixing desk. The move was apparently made to accommodate the new change in sound evident on It's Written in the Stars (but not apparent elsewhere) but was more likely because Weller had grown tired with the amount of time Lynch spent mixing. However, where *Heliocentric*'s looseness means it drags in its mid-section, *Illumination* refuses to slow down. As if the energy in its recording was spurred on by alcohol, where *Heliocentric*'s was held back by weed. Which in both cases, was probably not far from the truth.

First track Going Places hits the ground running, with Weller playing acoustic guitar, rather than his trademark Epiphone, in order to offer an outdoorsey sound. Track two, A Bullet for Everyone, is classic riff-laden Weller, taking influence from early seventies Stones, the central lumpy guitar line supported by an excellent Hammond organ and guitar feedback as well a one of Weller's best solos in years. Quite why track three Leafy Mysterious was chosen as the second and last single from the album, rather than the former track is a complete mystery.

Aside from the excellent brass loop on It's Written in the Stars, Dine's role as producer isn't obvious on every track and it is Weller that understandably dominates, his four-to-the-floor production style giving no quarter. The tracks lurch onto the next before the memory of the previous one is allowed to fade.

The acoustic is back out on Who Brings Joy, a slow ballad dedicated to Weller's daughter, "I just want so much to be there for you" and supported by some wonderous backing vocals from Weller himself. Now the Night is Here, the only other song credited to Dine, also uses the acoustic (it's on every track), and sounds so sixties and seventies, it could have been played by any act from the Mamas and the Papas to Lynyrd Skynyrd but is otherwise unremarkable.

Like all of Weller's later work, it isn't necessarily about the individual songs, but rather the feel of it, and bits of song stick out more than whole tracks such as the Simon Dine-penned brass intro to Spring

(At Last), that also features ex-Stone Roses and Ian Brown guitarist Aziz Ibrahim on the Indian instrument sarod; the lovely electronic piano line to All Good Books; or the inclusion of the co-authored, call and response duet with Kelly Jones from Stereophonics. The blues-rock of Call Me No. 5, surely one of the album's highpoints, juxtaposes nicely with the mostly acoustic plodders that make up the second half of the album.

Illumination may have signalled the end of recording this way for Weller, but the album's individuality was distinct enough to give it its own identity, as well as making sure that it fit perfectly into his canon. Something may have ended in 2002, but one thing was for sure, the Modfather was back.

Single 21:

Leafy Mysteries
Released: 18th November 2002; UK Chart Position: 23; Label: Independiente; Album: *Illumination*
B-sides: CD1: Talisman; Wild Wood*
CD2: Leafy Mysteries*; Broken Stones*; Peacock Suit*

*recorded live in Hyde Park, London, 28th July 2002

UK Official Singles Chart – Top 10 – 24th November 2002:

1. Dirrty – Christina Aguilera ft. Redman
2. Don't Let Me Down/You and I – Will Young
3. Jenny From the Block – Jennifer Lopez
4. Dilemma – Nelly ft. Kelly Rowland

5. Alive – S Club
6. The Ketchup Song (Asereje) – Las Ketchup
7. Heaven – DJ Sammy and Yanou ft. Do
8. Through the Rain – Mariah Carey
9. Stronger/Angels with Dirty Faces – Sugababes
10. Unbreakable – Westlife

....

23. Leafy Mysteries – Paul Weller

The release of Leafy Mysteries rounded off a great year for Weller in 2002. Despite the single only reaching number 23, the album had done better than expected, and Weller could take the time to relax and once again reflect on what would be his next move.

There would be no new Weller compositions until 2005's *As Is Now*, also recorded in Gallagher's Wheeler End Studios. Before that there would be his 2004 album of covers, *Studio 150*, and before even that, the requisite B-sides and rarities album.

Fly on the Wall: B-sides & Rarities

With *Illumination* and *Days of Speed* doing good business for Weller and for Independiente in 2002, Island decided to cash in during the quiet period in 2003 and released *Fly on the Wall – B-sides & Rarities*, three CDs worth of stuff that Weller fans couldn't get anywhere else (except on the internet...), all recorded between 1991 and 2001.

Alongside the very listenable demos of tracks like Into Tomorrow, and remixes of the likes of Wild Wood by Portishead, there was also some great material only available on the flip sides of some of the early singles, such as Here's a New Thing or The Loved, the latter of which he had played live on *Days of Speed*, but here appears in its original full band format. Whilst the inclusion of instrumental tracks such as That Spiritual Feeling or So You Want to be a Dancer remind us that Weller is about more than just the vocal and guitar.

The first two CDs are mostly Weller compositions, or those attributed to the various members of his band, whilst CD3 is made up of the many covers that he also included on his B-sides, or played live, including two Beatles' tracks, one John Lennon solo, a Bob Dylan track, a Neil Young one, and several drawn from his extensive soul collection. And there is even a track by Ben Harper (by far the most contemporary artist – despite being born in 1969).

B-sides Album:

Fly on the Wall: B Sides & Rarities
Released: 25th August 2003; UK Chart Position: 22; Label: Island
Track Listing: CD1: Here's A New Thing; That Spiritual Feeling (Lee/Nelson/Talbot); Into Tomorrow (Demo); Arrival Time (Peake/White); Fly On The Wall; Always There To Fool You; All Year Round; Ends Of The Earth; This Is No Time (Nelson); Another New Day (Lynch/White); Foot Of The Mountain (live); Wild Wood (Portishead Remix); Kosmos (Lynch Mob Bonus Beats Remix)
CD2: The Loved; Steam (Lynch); It's A New Day Baby; A Year Late; Eye Of The Storm (Nelson/White); Shoot The Dove; As You Lean Into The Light; So You Want To Be A Dancer (Lynch/Nelson/Deighton/White); Everything Has A Price To Pay; Right Underneath It; Helioscentric; There's No Drinking After You're

Dead (Noonday Underground Remix); The Riverbank; Science (Lynch Mob Remix)
CD3: Feelin' Alright (Mason); Ohio (Young); Black Sheep Boy (Hardin); Sexy Sadie (Lennon/McCartney); I Shall Be Released (Dylan); I'd Rather Go Blind (Foster/Jordan); My Whole World Is Falling Down (Crutcher/Jones); Ain't No Love In The Heart Of The City (Walsh/Price); Waiting On An Angel (Harper); Bang-Bang (Bono); Instant Karma (Lennon); Don't Let Me Down (Lennon/McCartney)
Producer/s: Paul Weller; Brendan Lynch

UK Official Albums Chart – Top 10 – 31st August 2003:

1. *Permission to Land* – The Darkness
2. *American Tune* – Eva Cassidy
3. *Take Them On, On your Own* – the Black Rebel Motorcycle Club
4. *Busted* – Busted
5. *Dutty Rock* – Sean Paul
6. *Gotta Get Thru This* – Daniel Bedingfield
7. *Escapology* – Robbie Williams
8. *Love and Life* – Mary J. Blige
9. *Youth and Young Manhood* – Kings of Leon
10. *Innocent Eyes* – Delta Goodrem

....

22. *Fly on the Wall: B Sides & Rarities* – *Paul Weller*

The top 10 albums chart in August 2003 shows a musical landscape more open than it had been for some time. At number 1 for the first of a four-week run was *Permission to Land* by The Darkness. Once deemed a novelty act, the contemporary hair-metal act had been taken seriously as artists (with tongue firmly in cheek of course) when they had sold out the Astoria without having a record deal. Their debut album would eventually sell more than 1.2million copies, going x4 platinum[xxiii].

Alongside them, indie-dirge heroes Black Rebel Motor-
cycle Club were proving that you could make music that sounded like you were on both heroin and LSD at the same time and still turn it into a hit, with their second album, *Take Them On, On Your Own*. Meanwhile teen-poppers Busted, who were so far removed from BRMC they were in essence photographic negatives of them, were about to become the biggest band in the country. *Busted*, their self-titled debut, would remain in the charts for 74 weeks, but would never reach higher than number 2.

At the other end of the top 10 was the debut from American rockers Kings of Leon, who in a few years' time would be the only rock act left to score a hit album in the late noughties. All this, and Daniel Bedingfield. What's not to love?

CHAPTER SIX
Studio 150, As Is Now, Catch-Flame! and *Hit Parade* (2004-2006)

Another year, and yet another record deal. Weller signed to V2 in July 2003, hanging around for a relatively long period of time, releasing three records over the course of four years. V2 was founded by Richard Branson in 1996 after he was forced to sell the original Virgin Records (who had famously signed the Sex Pistols, and kept them!), in order to save Virgin Airways. V2 had hit the ground running by signing Stereophonics as their very first act, and the band went on to become one of the biggest Welsh acts ever. Latterly V2 also signed, amongst others: Elbow, Phoenix, Tom Jones, the Jesus and Mary Chain, Madness, Underworld, Moby and The White Stripes, and were folded into Universal in 2007.

Weller's first release for his new label was the aforementioned *Studio 150*. The album, named after the studio in Amsterdam in which he recorded it, was a selection of cover versions of songs by the likes of Bob Dylan, Neil Young and even a Noel Gallagher track, One Way Road. None of the tracks had been recorded or played by Weller before, and the album was intended to showcase an array of his musical influences, and just what he could do reimagine another song writer's music in his own style. The sprightly Gallagher, who was 37 when the album came out, was the youngest artist to have his work covered, by some considerable way.

The album was preceded by two singles, Gil Scott-Heron's The Bottle, in June 2004, and Wishing on a Star, originally performed by the American soul group Rose Royce, in August that same year. Both were top 20 hits, signalling that Weller's new direction was going to be accepted by his fans.

Single 22:

The Bottle (Scott-Heron)
Released: 14th June 2004; UK Chart Position: 13; Label: V2; Album: *Studio 150*
B-sides: Corrina, Corrina (Chatman/Williams/Michell); Coconut Grove (Sebastian/Yanovsky)

UK Official Singles Chart – Top 10 – 20th June 2004:

1. Everytime – Britney Spears
2. I Don't Wanna Know – Mario Winans ft. Enya and P. Diddy
3. Come On England – 4-4-2
4. Dragostea Din Tei – O-Zone
5. Trick Me – Kelis
6. Talk About Our Love – Brandy ft. Kanye West
7. With You – Jessica Simpson
8. Hotel – Cassidy ft. R Kelly
9. Golden Touch – Razorlight
10. F.U.R.B. (F U Right Back) – Frankee

……………………………………..

13. The Bottle – Paul Weller

Aside from the inclusion of Razorlight's second wave of Britpop anthem Golden Touch, the only notable track in the top 10 in June 2004 was F.U.R.B. (F U Right Back) by Frankee. The song was released twice in 2004, eventually reaching number 1 in March, and was noted because of its use of the same backing track, but different vocal line to the song F**k It (I Don't Want you Back) by Eamon, which had also reached the top spot in April of the same year.

Frankee had claimed to be Eamon's ex and was apparently using his own song as a way of getting back at him for telling the world that he didn't want her back. However, Eamon later admitted that he did not even know Frankee and had only interacted with her in order to clear the rights to his track. Whichever version is true, neither party emerges from the sorry event looking particularly glorious, and the whole thing reeked of a horrendous publicity stunt. Luckily for the world, both acts quickly disappeared with no further hits to either of their names.

Single 23:

Wishing on a Star (Billie Rae Calvin)
Released: 30th August 2004; UK Chart Position: 11; Label: V2; Album: *Studio 150*
B-sides: Family Affair (Stewart); Let It Be Me (Becaud/Curtis/Delanoe)

UK Official Singles Chart – Top 10 – 5th September 2004:

1. My Place/Flap Your Wings – Nelly
2. Leave (Get Out) – Jojo
3. Sunshine – Twista
4. These Words – Natasha Bedingfield
5. Baby Cakes – 3 of a Kind
6. Dumb – 411
7. Gravity – Embrace
8. You Should Really Know – Pirates ft. Enya, Ama, Boss & Ishani

9. She Will Be Loved – Maroon 5

10. Guns Don't Kill People Rappers Do – Goldie Lookin Chain

....

11. Wishing on a Star – Paul Weller

If you're going to be beaten to the top 10, then finding yourself nudged out by the Goldie Lookin Chain is no big deal. The comedy Welsh rap group, who had courted much media attention by signing their major label deal (with Atlantic Records) in front of the Houses of Parliament in 2004, experienced some short lived mainstream success with this single, Guns Don't Kill People Rappers Do (which reached number 3), and its corresponding album, the slightly misleadingly named *Greatest Hits*, before disappearing off into self-imposed obscurity. They are still together today, have released a staggering 24 albums to date, and have something of a revolving door membership.

Album 7:

Studio 150
Released: 14th September 2004; UK Chart Position: 2; Label: V2
Track Listing: If I Could Only Be Sure (Gabriel Mekler, Nolan Porter); Wishing on a Star (Billie Rae Calvin); Don't Make Promises (Tim Hardin); The Bottle (Gill Scott-Heron); Black is the Colour (trad.); Close to You (Burt Bacharach, Hal David); Early Morning Rain (Gordon Lightfoot); One Way Road (Noel Gallagher); Hercules (Allen Toussaint); Thinking of You (Bernard Edwards, Nile Rodgers); All Along the Watchtower (Bod Dylan); Birds (Neil Young)

Producer/s: Paul Weller; Jan Kybert

UK Official Albums Chart – Top 10 – 19th September 2004:

1. *Out of Nothing* – Embrace
2. ***Studio 150* – Paul Weller**
3. *Unwritten* – Natasha Bedingfield
4. *Songs About Jane* – Maroon 5
5. *Greatest Hits* – Goldie Lookin Chain
6. *Hopes and Fears* – Keane
7. *Solarized* – Ian Brown
8. *Suit* – Nelly
9. *Let's Bottle Bohemia* – The Thrills
10. *Up All Night* – Razorlight

Just pipped to the top spot by former label mates Embrace, who were experiencing another lease of life with their fourth album *Out of Nothing, Studio 150* went straight in at number 2, Weller's third album to do so, after *Wild Wood* and *Heavy Soul.*

Embrace had started their career strongly, their 1998's debut *The Good Will Out* reaching number 1, but the following years had seen their success wain. That was until the man of the hour Chris Martin penned their comeback single Gravity, and the corresponding album became their second number 1, and most successful album to date.

Studio 150

The key thing that Weller's avid audience can take away from the *Studio 150* album is a better understanding of their hero's taste in music. In many ways it's like a mix-tape, or a DJ set, in which Weller tries to express himself through other people's music. It's not for the first time of course, Weller has never been shy about the type of music that inspires him (and the type that doesn't...), and has often included covers of much loved tracks as B-sides, played them live, or in the case of Walk on Gilded Splinters, even reserved a key spot on a key album. Each time he pays homage to his favourite artists, offering them respect for helping him create the music that he does.

Studio 150 is slightly different though. Rather than simply compiling the songs that he loves, Weller has chosen 12 tracks that he feels he (and his band) can really do justice to. Which means the album ranges from the obscure (Black is the Colour) to the ultra-popular (Close to You), or in other words, from the sublime to the ridiculous. Yet the final result is so Weller, it only really makes sense once listened to. If, like your author, you were initially reticent about listening to a Weller covers album, go put the album on right now! It's quite simply amazing.

Things get under way on familiar ground with Nolan Porter's If I Could Only Be Sure. It's the type of song you would expect Weller to cover, traditional American soul transposed to the right key for his gravelly voice, and layered with guitar and keyboard licks and his favourite four-four drumbeat. Porter was an American R'n'B singer who was best known for the Northern Soul anthem Keep on Keeping On, which was later used by Joy Division as the basis for their track Interzone, released on *Unknown Pleasures* in 1979. Nolan released just two albums during his seventies tenure, but experienced something of a career renaissance thanks to Weller's cover, and the pair kept in contact, even playing together as recently as 2015, on stage at the Fonda Theatre in Los Angeles, performing Heatwave.

By track 2 though, we're already heading into uncharted territory with the album's second single, Wishing on a Star. Written by Billie Rae Calvin and performed initially by Rose Royce, the song was probably best known in its 1992 version by the Cover Girls. The reedy, whimsical song should be out of place in Weller's oeuvre but takes on a matter-of-fact quality due to his unsentimental delivery. The song was also very current, having been released as recently as 1998, as a rap version by Jay-Z, who recorded with Gwen Dickey from Rose Royce. And Mr. Z's wife Beyonce included her version of the song on her *Live at Wembley* album, played in 2004, but not released until September 2005, so sandwiching Weller's version between the two. Yet again, Weller managed to make himself seem incredibly current, whilst remaining totally rooted in the time and style that he loves the most.

Gil Scott-Heron's The Bottle, a number 13 hit back in June 2004, and Weller's first release for V2, is a raucous foot-stomper heavily indebted to Scott-Heron (obviously), Curtis Mayfield and all northern soul, the brass refrain disguising a song which is only a thinly veiled confession of alcoholism: "Where is the man I was?, And not this black eyed dog, Who barks away at night", not Weller's first time covering this subject matter.

It is likely that Weller first heard the traditional Scottish folk song Black is the Colour via Nina Simone's 1959 version, although Joan Baez also covered it around the same time, and Weller's version is added to a long list of artists who have played it. Weller isn't often associated with folk music, but this faithful version is suitably supported by Eliza Carthy's incredibly folky violin (she also plays on Early Morning Rain).

Things quite easily could have fallen apart with Weller's decision to cover Burt Bacharach's corny classic Close to You (remember Alan Partridge singing it on Valentine's Day to Gill?), but this version is almost unrecognisable, Weller playing around with the melody enough to create an altogether different version, which is as refreshing as it is surprising.

There are a few fillers on the album that would have probably been more at home as B-sides, Early Morning Rain and Don't Make Promises are fine but nothing special, but it is on the only song composed after 1990 that Weller saves the real magic. Of all of the classic songs written by Noel Gallagher, Weller chooses to cover a B-side from the least respected era of Oasis' illustrious career, the *Standing on the Shoulder of Giants* period. And the B-side to second single, Who Feels Love?, One Way Road. Weller transforms the track, turning it into a modern soul corker, with a huge chorus and beautiful brass refrain, Carleen Anderson's incendiary backing vocals pushing the track up to the next level. He also makes it sound like the song was written in 1966, which probably would have impressed Mr. Gallagher very much.

Two of the most well-known artists to provide songs for the album are Bob Dylan and Neil Young, both major influences on Weller, and both versions of their songs are great, but it is the Nile Rodgers penned Thinking of You that chimed the most with audiences (3.3million plays on Spotify, to Dylan's All Along the Watchtower's 235k[xxiv]).

Made famous by Sister Sledge in 1984, but first released as the flipside to the disco classic Lost in Music in 1978, the song has a universality outside of its disco trappings that Weller brings to the fore with his full band version. He adds strings, familiar to the original, frantically strums his acoustic, harmonises with himself, Steve White and the band only entering halfway through, and then slowly builds to a repeated coda that feels like it could go on forever. It's a moment of true bliss, and an apt way to bring about the beginning of the end of the record.

Studio 150 was an incredibly expensive way to record a mix-tape, but peaking at number 2 in the charts meant that it would have at least given something back, and most importantly it showed Weller's audience yet another side to what he could do as a recording artist. That audience had proved themselves loyal, but not blindly so (a lesson learned through the *Heliocentric* phase), and Weller would need to keep reinventing himself if he was to remain a vibrant and current artist over the coming years. His next move, well, that was take a step back, of course.

Single 24:

Thinking of You (Rodgers/Edwards)
Released: 15th November 2004; UK Chart Position: 18; Label: V2; Album: *Studio 150*
B-sides: Don't Go to Strangers (Kent/Mann/Evans); Needles and Pins (Nitzsche/Bono)

UK Official Singles Chart – Top 10 – 21st November 2004:

1. I'll Stand by You – Girls Aloud
2. Lose My Breath – Destiny's Child
3. If There's Any Justice – Lemar
4. What You Waiting For – Gwen Stefani
5. Room on the 3rd Floor – McFly

6. Just Lose It – Eminem
7. Vertigo – U2
8. Baby It's You – Jojo ft. Bow Wow
9. Confessions Part II/My Boo – Usher
10. Car Wash – Christina Aguilera ft. Missy Elliot

…………………………………………

18. Thinking of You – Paul Weller

<u>Single 25:</u>

Early Morning Rain (Lightfoot)
Released: 14th March 2005; UK Chart Position: 40;
Label: V2; Album: *Studio 150*
B-sides: Come Together (Lennon/McCartney)

UK Official Singles Chart – Top 10 – 20th March 2005:

1. (Is This The Way To) Amarillo – Tony Christie ft. Peter Kay
2. All About You/You've Got a Friend – McFly
3. She's Not You – Elvis Presley
4. Rich Girl – Gwen Stefani ft. Eve
5. Falling Stars – Sunset Strippers
6. They – Jem
7. Over and Over – Nelly ft. Tim McGraw
8. Oh My Gosh – Basement Jaxx
9. Bohemian Rhapsody – G4
10. Back to Basics – Shapeshifters

…………………………………………

40. Early Morning Rain – Paul Weller

Despite having been dead for 27 years, Elvis Presley was still releasing records and She's Not You was new at number 3 in March 2005, just as Weller released the fourth and final single from *Studio 150*,

Gordon Lightfoot's understated Early Morning Rain. Unsurprisingly, the troubadour's rumbling acoustic track was at total odds with the top 10 the week it charted, despite the chart also featuring Tony Christie alongside Elvis, and even a cover of the Beatles' latter day classic Come Together on the B-side couldn't help push the single any further than number 40.

It was probably an unnecessary single to be released but it rounded off the covers album project nicely, and paved the way for Weller's return to composition, with his next album *As Is Now*, and its raucously catchy lead single, From the Floorboards Up.

Back to Basics

Just as the final single from *Studio 150* was clawing its way into the top 40, Weller was back in Noel's Wheeler End Studio to record his next album of originals, October 2005's *As Is Now*. Despite being his lowest charting album since his debut (reaching number 4), *As Is Now* was generally well accepted by fans and critics alike, and was notable for its return to the rock 'n' roll that everyone loved from Weller, particularly the aforementioned single, which would be Weller's highest charting one since Peacock Suit, all the way back in 1996.

Single 26:

From the Floorboards Up
Released: 18th July 2005; UK Chart Position: 6; Label: V2; Album: *As Is Now*
B-sides: Oranges and Rosewater; From the Floorboards Up (video)

UK Official Singles Chart – Top 10 – 24th July 2005:

1. You're Beautiful – James Blunt
2. We Belong Together – Mariah Carey
3. Army of Lovers – Lee Ryan
4. Ghetto Gospel – 2Pac ft. Elton John
5. Gasolina – Daddy Yankee
6. **From the Floorboards Up – Paul Weller**
7. Since U Been Gone – Kelly Clarkson
8. Crazy Chick – Charlotte Church
9. Roc Ya Body (Mic Check 1 2) – MVP
10. Axel F – Crazy Frog

Another act who was good at releasing singles, despite having died nearly ten years earlier, was Tupac Shakur (or 2Pac), at number 4 in July 2005, with the massive single Ghetto Gospel, which sampled Elton John's Indian Sunset. Of the eighteen 2Pac singles that have made the top 100 in the UK, just three of them were released before he died in September 1996. As an artist, Shakur was incredibly prolific, and it would have been fascinating to see what he would have come up with had he managed to keep on recording.

As for the number 1 in late July 2005, You're Beautiful was a massive hit for former military man James Blunt. In 2019 the single was certified twice platinum, meaning it has sold more than 1.2million copies[xxv]. It remained at the top spot for five weeks and played a major part in Blunt's debut album *Back to Bedlam* going x5 platinum by the end of 2005, selling more than 1.5million copies[xxvi]. By November 2014 the album had gone x11 platinum (3.3million sales)[xxvii], making it the biggest selling album of the noughties.

It isn't hard to guess what Weller would have to say about Blunt, and the enormous success of such vapid pop music speaks volumes about the temperate tastes of the British record buying public in 2005. Blunt himself isn't without a sense of humour though, and is only too aware of the disposable nature of his songs. He tweeted at the end of 2016, a year that saw the loss of David Bowie, Prince, George Michael, and many others, "If you thought 2016 was bad – I'm releasing an album in 2017.[xxviii]"

Single 27:

Come On/ Let's Go
Released: 26th September 2005; UK Chart Position: 15; Label: V2; Album: *As Is Now*
B-sides: Shine On; Come On/ Let's Go (video)

UK Official Singles Chart – Top 10 – 2nd October 2005:

1. Push the Button – Sugababes
2. Don't Cha – Pussycat Dolls ft. Busta Rhymes
3. We Be Burnin' – Sean Paul
4. Gold Digger – Kanye West ft. Jamie Foxx
5. Song 4 Lovers – Liberty X
6. Bad Day – Daniel Power
7. Nine Million Bicycles – Katie Melua
8. All About Us – Tatu
9. Doctor Pressure – Mylo vs. Miami Sound Machine
10. Call My Name – Charlotte Church

…………………………………………………

15. Come On/ Let's Go – Paul Weller

Album 8:

As Is Now
Released: 11th October 2005; UK Chart Position: 4; Label: V2
Track Listing: Blink and You'll Miss It; Paper Smile; Come On/ Let's Go; Here's the Good News; The Start is Forever; Pan; All on a Misty Morning; From the Floorboards Up; I Wanna Make it Alright; Savages; Fly Little Bird; Roll Along Summer; Bring Back the Funk (parts 1&2); The Pebble and the Boy
Producer/s: Paul Weller; Jan Kybert

UK Official Albums Chart – Top 10 – 16th October 2005:

1. *Taller in More Ways* – Sugababes
2. *Back to Bedlam* – James Blunt
3. *Piece by Piece* – Katie Melua
4. ***As Is Now* – Paul Weller**
5. *You Could Have It So Much Better* – Franz Ferdinand
6. *Eye to the Telescope* – KT Tunstall
7. *Life in Slow Motion* – David Gray
8. *Breakaway* – Kelly Clarkson
9. *Greatest Hits* – Mariah Carey
10. *Simple Gifts* – Bryn Terfel

Aside from Sugababes and Franz Ferdinand, all of the acts in the top 10 in October 2005 were solo artists, and the same 10 was split exactly equally between female and male acts. Weller's eighth studio album may have only reached number 4, but it would spend six weeks on the chart, before returning for another run in early 2006, eventually going gold (100k units sold), by February 2006[xxix].

As Is Now

Aptly summed up in the name of its first track, Blink and You'll Miss It, *As Is Now* was recorded in just two weeks and is an urgent, passionate album that finds Weller leaning more toward the guitar rock of *Heavy Soul* and *Illumination*, and away from the blue-eyed soul of his debut. The decision to record the album with such immediacy was made on purpose, Paul telling Steve White, "he wanted to write a record that sounded like one continual piece", and, "it was [producer Jan] Kybert's idea to record the band as soon as possible after they had been touring together"[xxx].

Blink and You'll Miss It is as good an opening track as any of his albums, setting the tone for the guitar led indie-rock that is to follow. Paper Smile is a song that picks up John Lennon's message of life being what happens when you're making other plans, and finds Weller dabbling once more in the themes of disillusionment began in the seventies and those early Jam records, but with a *Stanley Road* era guitar sound washing over Steve White's persistent drums.

Second single Come On/ Let's Go also sounds like a Jam song, like Strange Town played by The Undertones, and refuses to let the tempo drop lower than Blink and You'll Miss It first set ten minutes earlier. There are few flourishes or much studio invention (again, it was recorded in just two weeks), and each track stalks from one to the next without letting up for a minute, as if Weller is planning on winning his audience over when he plays the album live. A smart move as it would turn out, and *Catch-*

Flame, his third live album, would be released in June 2006, having been recorded the last night of the *As Is Now* tour in December 2005.

Had Blink and You'll Miss It been left off the album, then keeping back the excellent first single From the Floorboards Up until track 8 might have been an odd move, but as it is, Weller's ultimate party tune starts off the second half of the album in fine fettle. As he told Ian Snowball:

> *It's a song about playing live to an audience where, on a good night, the power seems to come up from the ground through the stage, through the band and out into the audience where the energy hangs in the air. You can't see it but boy, you feel it.*[xxxi]

Whether the album needed 14 tracks is another matter, and To the Start of Forever and Pan, fine songs for sure, might have been better placed as B-sides. But then that's not really the point. *As Is Now*, just as its title suggests, is Weller at his most current. If *Studio 150* laid out his influences from the previous 50 years, then *As Is Now* aims to capture exactly what he sounds like in this one moment in time. And this is most certainly does.

With *As Is Now* being recorded whilst *Studio 150* was still within its lifespan (both albums were mixed at Studio 150), the two albums are two sides of the same coin, and they let Weller express the two sides of himself in different ways. At 47, he was closing in on his half century, more set in his ways than ever before but also more aware of who he is, and more able to express himself than he had ever been able to previously. If there is a theme to the album then it seems to be about not letting life slip by without enjoying it and, on I Wanna Make it Alright, he even offers some form of regret for what feels like the first time, saying to the song's unknown subject, "I wanna put things right on this ground, before our time is through".

Where the first half of the record notable for its guitar heavy chords and overdriven riffs, the second half is much more mellow, yet no less intense. The minor chord acoustic guitars and pounding pianos lead songs with striking, evocative names like Savages or the restrained ballad Fly Little Bird, a song that seems to echo the themes of escape and quest for freedom apparent in McCartney's Blackbird.

After the upbeat Bring Back the Funk (Parts 1 & 2), the album comes to its conclusion with the melodic The Pebble and the Boy, a drawn out ballad with overpowering strings, that reminds of the feel but not the style of one of Weller's best tracks, Broken Stones, from *Stanley Road*. It also showcases Weller's piano playing, which in turn reminds us what a naturally gifted musician he is, and surely one that is just entering the height of his powers.

Single 28:

Here's the Good News
Released: 5th December 2005; UK Chart Position: 21; Label: V2; Album: *As Is Now*
B-sides: Super Lekker Stoned (Richard Fearless Remix)

UK Official Singles Chart – Top 10 – 11th December 2005:

1. Stickwitu – Pussycat Dolls

2. Hung Up – Madonna
3. Ugly – Sugababes
4. You Raise Me Up – Westlife
5. Juicebox – The Strokes
6. My Humps – Black Eyed Peas
7. Listen to Your Heart – DHT ft. Edmee
8. No Worries – Simon Webbe
9. Let There Be Love – Oasis
10. Because of You – Kelly Clarkson

....

21. Here's the Good News – Paul Weller

Not quite as terrible as it might look at first glance. The chart in December 2005 may have been filled with the likes of DHT ft. Edmee (nope, me neither), but were also populated with Let There Be Love, Oasis' most tender ballad, plus Franz Ferdinand were at 13 with Walk Away, Arctic Monkeys were at 14 (down from 1) with I Bet You Look Good on the Dancefloor, and Gorillaz were at 15 with Dirty Harry.

Weller just missed out on the top 20 with the jauntiest track on As Is Now, Here's the Good News (which is oddly reminiscent of Oasis' Kinks-like The Importance of Being Idle, number 1 in August 2005), no huge surprise considering it was the third single from the album.

So, What Next?

With *As Is Now* out in the world doing its thing, Weller started to tour again. The album had been launched with a gig at HMV on Oxford Street (at the time, the country's biggest record store), and a week later he was off to Europe for a handful of dates throughout October, then back to the UK for

November, finishing up playing a massive concert at Alexandra Palace in North London on 5th December.

It was this gig that provided the setting for his next live album, *Catch-Flame!* (its title taken from a lyric in You Do Something to Me) released in July 2006. The two CD concert album was made up of tracks from across Weller's whole career including, for the first time, songs by The Style Council, such as Long Hot Summer and Shout to the Top. The best moments of his solo career, The Changingman, Blink and You'll Miss It, were spliced together with classic Jam songs, That's Entertainment and set closer Town Called Malice, and alongside near-forgotten gems, like In the Crowd from *All Mod Cons*. The concert also included an acoustic set, featuring Wishing on a Star, You Do Something to Me and Wild Wood. A Weller fan's wet dream, to say the least.

This in turn (inevitably) fuelled the flames of retrospect and yet another best-of hit the record store shelves in November. *Hit Parade* was released by his old friends at Island and featured a picture of an early Jam era Weller on its front cover. The album went twice platinum and was released both as a single disc, and as a mammoth four-disc boxed set version. It reached number 7 in the charts. New track Wild Blue Yonder would be released as a single in order to help promote *Hit Parade*, although interestingly, it wouldn't be included on either version of the album.

Another reason for these two major retrospectives was that on 14th February, Valentine's Day, 2006, Weller was (finally) awarded the lifetime achievement award by the Brits. Being awarded the year before Oasis, and two years before Paul McCartney (The Beatles were awarded back in 1983), was something of a fitting honour for Weller, and put him amongst such exalted company as George Martin, The Who, Rod Stewart, and Bob Geldof, who was given it the year before Weller, the latter of which must have stung considering Geldof's lack of musical output in comparison. It was a fitting tribute to a great artist, and he played a short set that included The Changingman, From the Floorboards Up, and Town Called Malice.

Live Album 3:

Catch-Flame!
Released: 25th July 2006; UK Chart Position: 17; Label: V2
Track Listing: CD1: The Weaver; Out of the Sinking; Blink and You'll Miss It; Paper Smile; Peacock Suit; From the Floorboards Up; The Changingman (Weller/Lynch); Savages; Going Places; Up in Suze's Room; Porcelain Gods/I Walk on Gilded Splinters (Creaux)
CD2: In the Crowd; Come On/ Let's Go; Foot of the Mountain; You Do Something to Me; Wishing on a Star (Calvin); Wild Wood; The Pebble and the Boy; That's Entertainment; Broken Stones; Long Hot Summer; Shout to the Top; Town Called Malice
Producer/s: Paul Weller; Jan Kybert

UK Official Albums Chart – Top 10 – 18th June 2006:

1. *Under the Iron Sea* – Keane
2. *Smile It Confuses People* – Sandi Thom
3. *Twelve Stops and Home* – The Feeling
4. *Surprise* – Paul Simon
5. *Loose* – Nelly Furtado

6. *Stadium Arcadium* – Red Hot Chili Peppers
7. *Inside In/ Inside Out* – The Kooks
8. *The Very Best Of* – Nine Simone
9. *The Complete Greatest Hits* – The Eagles
10. *Eyes Open* – Snow Patrol

……………………………………………

17. *Catch-Flame!* – Paul Weller

A relatively high proportion of indie-rock bands featured in the albums chart in July 2006, with Keane at number 1 with their second album *Under the Iron Sea*, plus debut long players from The Feeling, and The Kooks, and the massive selling number 1 fourth album from Snow Patrol (its second single Chasing Cars was the most played song on the radio in the UK in the 21st century[xxxii]), *Eyes Open*.

Weller's live album, definitely his best, but still not made up of new music, crept into the top 20 at number 17, one place behind Primal Scream's eighth album, *Riot City Blues*.

<u>Single 29:</u>

Wild Blue Yonder
Released: 6th November 2006; UK Chart Position: 22; Label: V2; Album: n/a
B-sides: Small Personal Fortune; The Start of Forever (acoustic)

<u>UK Official Singles Chart – Top 10 – 12th November 2006:</u>

1. The Rose – Westlife
2. The Saints are Coming – U2 & Green Day
3. Rock Steady – All Saints
4. Put Your Hands Up for Detroit –

Fedde le Grand

5. Irreplaceable – Beyonce
6. Yeah Yeah – Bodyrox ft. Luciana
7. Something Kinda Ooooh – Girls Aloud
8. Easy – Sugababes
9. Jump – Madonna
10. Welcome to the Black Parade – My Chemical Romance

……………………………………………………

22. Wild Blue Yonder – Paul Weller

Westlife were at number 1 in November 2006 with their fourteenth chart topper, The Rose. Overall, this puts the Irish boyband in third equal placing in UK chart history for most number 1 singles, behind Elvis (21), The Beatles (17), and tied with Cliff Richard, and one ahead of Madonna. Although, because The Beatles managed to score all of theirs within a seven-year period, surely they win.

Weller's single Wild Blue Yonder though peaked at number 22 and was released to help promote the *Hit Parade* collection that was released on the same day. The track is classic Weller and consists of pretty much just the title repeated over and over.

Best of Album no. 2:

Hit Parade
Released: 6th November 2006; UK Chart Position: 7; Label: Island
Track Listing: CD1: In the City; All Around the World; The Modern World; News of the World (Foxton); David Watts (Davis); 'A' Bomb in Wardour Street; Down in the Tube Station at Midnight; Strange Town; When You're Young; The Eton Rifles; Going Underground; Dreams of

Children; Start!; That's Entertainment; Funeral Pyre (Buckler/Foxton/Weller); Absolute Beginners; Town Called Malice; Precious; Just Who is the Five O'Clock Hero?; The Bitterest Pill (I Ever Had to Swallow); Beat Surrender
CD2: Speak Like a Child; Money Go Round; Long Hot Summer; Solid Bond In Your Heart; My Ever Changing Moods; You're Best Thing; Big Boss Groove (Talbot/Weller); Shout to the Top!; Walls Come Tumbling Down; Come to Milton Keynes; The Lodgers (Talbot/Weller); Have You Ever Had it Blue; It Didn't Matter (Talbot/Weller); Waiting; Wanted (Talbot/Weller); Life at a Top People's Health Farm (Talbot/Weller); How She Threw it Away; Promised Land (Smooth)
CD3: Into Tomorrow; Uh-Huh Oh-Yeh; Above the Clouds; Sunflower; Wild Wood; The Weaver; Hung Up; Out of the Sinking; The Changingman (Lynch/Weller); You Do Something to Me; Broken Stones; Peacock Suit; Brushed (Lynch/Nelson/Weller/White); Friday Street; Mermaids
CD4: Brand New Start; He's the Keeper; Sweet Pea, My Sweet Pea; It's Written in the Stars (Weller/Dine); Leafy Mysteries; The Bottle (Scott-Heron); Wishing on a Star (Calvin); Thinking of You (Edwards/Rodgers); Early Morning Rain (Lightfoot); From the Floorboards Up; Come On/ Let's Go!; Here's the Good News; Blink and You'll Miss It
Producer/s: Chris Parry; Vic Smith; Vic Coppersmith-Heaven; Peter Wilson; Mick Talbot; Brendan Lynch; Simon Dine; Jan Kybert; Paul Weller

UK Official Albums Chart – Top 10 – 12th November 2006:

1. *High Times – Singles 1992-2006* – Jamiroquai
2. *Angelis* – Angelis
3. *The Sound of – The Greatest Hits* – Girls Aloud
4. *9* – Damien Rice
5. *Serenade* – Katherine Jenkins
6. *Motion in the Ocean* – McFly
7. ***Hit Parade* – Paul Weller**
8. *Two's Company – The Duets* – Cliff Richard
9. *Rudebox* – Robbie Williams
10. *Back to Black* – Amy Winehouse

CHAPTER SEVEN
The Island Years Pt. 2 – *22 Dreams, Weller at the BBC,* and *Wake Up the Nation* (2007-2010)

In July 2007, Weller released the first of two duets, neither of which would appear on accompanying Weller albums. The first of these was with Graham Coxon, the erstwhile guitarist with Britpoppers Blur, who had been asked to leave his band back in 2003 but was experiencing something of a fruitful solo career. The pair had appeared on the same bill together back in April 2005, a fundraiser for the Japanese tsunami effort, and may have hooked up there.

This Old Town starts out like a classic solo Coxon track, perhaps a little bit retro, even for him, but quickly evolves into a great pop-rock song akin to the *As Is Now* era Weller. Coxon leads the track but Weller compliments him perfectly, with a harmony vocal on the chorus. The song deserved a higher placing than the 39 it eventually made.

The second duet was with another Blur affiliate, Andy Lewis, a DJ who specialised in sixties music (you can see how he got together with Weller), and who supported Blur on their *Parklife* tour. Are You Trying to be Lonely? is a perfect slice of northern soul, led by one of Lewis' trademark brass riffs, and featuring a vocal from Weller, that wouldn't have sounded out of place being sung by PP Arnold or even Diana Ross. It appeared on Lewis' 2007 album *You Should Be Hearing Something Now.*

The only other record that Weller would release in 2007 was the deluxe edition reissue of *Wild Wood,* in honour of its 14th birthday. The release peaked at number 88 in the albums chart, and included three CDs worth of material, various remixes and demo versions sitting alongside the original album tracks and B-sides.

Single 30:

This Old Town (Coxon/Weller)
Released: 2nd July 2007; UK Chart Position: 39*; Label: Regal Recordings; Album: n/a
B-sides: Each New Morning (Coxon); Black River

*the track reached its peak chart position on 11th August 2007

UK Official Singles Chart – Top 10 – 5th August 2007:

1. The Way I Are – Timbaland ft. Keri Hilson
2. Foundations – Kate Nash
3. Big Girls Don't Cry – Fergie
4. Umbrella – Rihanna ft. Jay-Z
5. With Every Heartbeat – Robyn with Kleerup
6. Do You Know – Enrique Iglesias
7. Dream Catch Me – Newtown Faulkner
8. Worried About Ray – Hoosiers
9. Song 4 Mutya (Out of Control) – Groove Armada
10. Hey There Delilah – Plain white T's

....

39. This Old Town – Paul Weller and Graham Coxon

Single 31:

Are You Trying to be Lonely? (Lewis/Weller)
Released: 10th September 2007; UK Chart
Position: 31; Label: Acid Jazz; Album: n/a
B-sides: Tell Me Once Again You Love Me (Lewis);
The Lazuli Affair (Lewis); Are You Trying to be
Lonely? (Lewis/Weller)

UK Official Singles Chart – Top 10 – 16th September 2007:

1. Beautiful Girls – Sean Kingston
2. Hey There Delilah – Plain White T's
3. Stronger – Kanye West
4. 1973 – James Blunt
5. Ayo Technology – 50 Cent/Timberlake/ Timbaland
6. Shut up and Drive – Rihanna
7. Sexy No No No – Girls Aloud
8. With Every Heartbeat – Robyn with Kleerup
9. The Way I Are – Timbaland ft. Keri Hilson
10. She's So Lovely – Scouting for Girls

....

31. Are You Trying to be Lonely? – Andy Lewis and Paul Weller

Anyone for a double?

Back on Island Records, 2008 became as eventful a year for Weller as 2007 was not. Firstly, he split with long term partner and mother of two of his children, Sammi. The pair had been together since 1995, the busiest period of Weller's career, which saw him change from struggling solo artist into national treasure. Weller wasn't one to dwell though, and the split – plus his impending 50th birthday – was what spurned him on to make what became his most ambitious solo project yet, the epic double album, *22 Dreams*.

Recorded between 2007 and 2008, at Paul's own Black Barn Studios, *22 Dreams* was a marked departure from its predecessors. Weller was keen to record an album like *Sgt. Pepper*, where all the tracks were linked, and listeners were encouraged to play the whole thing through in one go. It would also be his most collaborative record to date, with 11 of the 21 tracks co-credited, and a whole host of featured artists, including old friends Steve Cradock, Noel Gallagher and Simon Dine, as well as some new faces, Lewis Wharton, Andy Lewis and Graham Coxon.

It would also be the final album to feature Steve White atop the drum stool. On and off, White had played with Weller for 15 years by this point, by far his longest serving band member, and the parting was bittersweet.

Single 32:

Have You Made Up Your Mind/ Echoes Round the Sun (Weller/Gallagher)
Released: 26th May 2008; UK Chart Position: 19; Label: Island; Album: *22 Dreams*
B-sides: Rise and Fall

UK Official Singles Chart – Top 10 – 1st June 2008:

1. Take a Bow – Rihanna
2. That's Not My Name – the Ting Tings
3. Warwick Avenue – Duffy

4. 4 Minutes – Madonna ft. Justin Timberlake
5. Heartbreaker – Will I Am ft. Cheryl Cole
6. Black & Gold – Sam Sparro
7. Closer – Ne-Yo
8. Love in This Club – Usher ft. Young Jeezy
9. Cry for You – September
10. Wearing My Rolex – Wiley

....

19. Have You Made Up Your Mind/ Echoes Round the Sun – Paul Weller

Weller's first time in the top 20 for nearly three years, Have You Made up Your Mind/ Echoes Round the Sun was not only the first double A side single release of his solo career, but was also the lowest charting first single to be released from an album since Out of the Sinking back in 1994.

Not for the first time, Weller found himself amongst alien company in the charts in June 2008. The only act he had anything in common with were Coldplay, at 11 with Violet Hill. And Weller hated Coldplay.

The releases from his ninth studio album do have something in common with the top 10 in June 2008 though. *22 Dreams* is mostly collaborations, in just the same way that most of the artists in the chart that week all feature somebody else. Featuring was of course nothing new to pop music, but in the new millennium it seemed to become more and more common, as singers guest on each other's singles in an aim to raise their own profile in an increasingly crowded marketplace.

Album 9:

22 Dreams
Released: 2nd June 2008; UK Chart Position: 1; Label: Island
Track Listing: Light Nights; 22 Dreams (Weller/Dine); All I Wanna Do (Is Be With You); Have You Made Up Your Mind; Empty Ring (Weller/Dine); Invisible; Song For Alice (Weller/Dine/Cradock); Cold Moments; The Dark Pages of September Lead to the new Leaves of Spring (Weller/Dine); Black River; What Walk When You Can Run; Push it Along (Weller/Dine); A Dream Reprise (Weller/Dine); Echoes Round the Sun (Weller/Gallagher); One Bright Star (Weller/Dine); Lullaby Für Kinder; Where'er Ye Go; God; 111 (Weller/Dine/Cradock); Sea Spray (Weller/Hannah Andrews); Night Lights (Weller/Cradock/Charles Rees/Andrews)
Producer/s: Paul Weller; Simon Dine; Steve Cradock; Charles Rees

UK Official Albums Chart – Top 10 – 8th June 2008:

1. ***22 Dreams* – Paul Weller**
2. *Rockferry* – Duffy
3. *Home Before Dark* – Neil Diamond
4. *The Best of* – Radiohead
5. *Here I Stand* – Usher
6. *You Can Do Anything* – the Zutons
7. *The Best of* – Neil Diamond
8. *We Started Nothing* – the Ting Tings
9. *Jumping All Over the World* – Scooter
10. *This is Alphabeat* – Alphabeat

A good week for Neil Diamond, with two albums in the top 10, in fact, a casual glance at the albums chart in June 2008 and you might confuse it for one in 1967. Weller at number 1 (somehow only his third solo number 1 album), plus the sixties style Welsh singer Duffy at number 2, Diamond of course, and then further down the chart the third album from Liverpool's Zutons (them of Valerie fame), *You Can Do Anything.*

22 Dreams

Every great artist needs to record a double album at some point in their career. And with *22 Dreams* it was apparently Weller's turn. The album opens with a folk song, not an alien genre to Weller, but certainly not slap band in centre of his wheelhouse, so, immediately we know this is going to be a different album than a simple set of songs strung together. Light Nights features just Weller and Hannah Anderson (who would become Mrs Weller a few years later) on b/v's, as well as the requisite Gaelic violin, and sets the tone for the album in as much as it states that this is not going to be an ordinary recording, but Weller's go at doing *The White Album.* Although it was actually *Sgt. Pepper* he was trying to emulate, he just got carried away.

The album had come about in something of a strange manner. Some months before it was recorded, Weller had quit the music business. Steve Cradock explains:

> *Out of the blue one day, Paul phoned me and said he wasn't going to make music anymore... He basically told me that he'd had enough of it. It lasted for about two*

months and then he phoned again asking if I'd go and do some demos with him.[xxxiii]

Those demoes turned into *22 Dreams*, and what started as just Weller and Cradock soon spiralled into a cast of thousands, with five credited songwriters, and twenty-four credited musicians, one of whom was God, Himself. It was actually Aziz Ibrahim, who had once upon a time replaced John Squire in The Stone Roses, and here provided the voice of God because, according to Weller, God was a Manc, and Noel Gallagher refused to do it.

Even more surprising though was the appearance for the first time since 1976 of Steve Brookes, Weller's old school friend and former member of The Jam, who played Spanish guitar on One Bright Star. This tells us that Weller was in something of an introspective place with his ambitions with the album. Just turned 50, newly single, children growing up, it was time to take stock, and *22 Dreams* was his way of expressing himself and looking back at the last half a century. He surrounds himself with friends old and new, and really lets the creative juices flow, perhaps more than at any point in his career.

With this in mind, the songs on the album tumble together one after the other in a joyous flow of free form pop music. The title track is an upbeat blast of northern soul, co-written with Simon Dine, Weller's closest production partner during this phase in his career. And subject-wise, it is not hard to see how Weller was trying to move on from his recent breakup and claim some sense of self.

I had 22 dreams last night
And you were in 21
The last one I saved for myself

Just to save my soul

A feeling that is at total odds with the sentiment of the next track, the slower, but emotionally more poignant All I Wanna Do (Is Be With You). The lyric is more complex than the title might suggest though ("I'm not here to forgive you, I'm neither clever nor confused"), and the song itself seems to marry Golden Years era Bowie with Paul's own *Stanley Road*. It's one of the album's high-lights. Which is not an easy statement to make on an album so densely packed with classic after classic Weller track.

There's also something of a seventies Bowie feel to first single Have You Made Up Your Mind, but the lyric and the sentiment to the song are all Weller, and the backing vocals in the chorus, which sound like Hannah Andrews, are actually Paul's right hand man Steve Cradock. Empty Ring returns the album to the early days of Weller's career, and the beautiful piano line and rolling strings remind of Weller's good friend Dr Robert's band The Blow Monkeys. Eighties favourites who channelled the sixties so perfectly into their dreamy disco-pop.

Dark piano ballads like Invisible push the album in another direction, and are beautifully juxtaposed amidst an album so prominently propped up by the likes of Empty Ring and the dark and stormy Song for Alice (dedicated to the jazz musician Alice Coltrane who died in January 2007).

It is in fact the album's eclecticism that makes it such a success. This can be a dangerous move for a band. Mansun, for example, partly lost their way with their second album *Six* because it was so eclectic, but Weller's years of experience meant that with *22 Dreams* he remained in the driving seat throughout. No sooner has one musical genre been covered than its time to leap on to the next one. Song for Alice gives way to the change of pace of Cold Moments, as if Weller has suddenly remembered that he needs to get some acoustic picking on the album.

Not every track is a classic pop song though, and just like *The White Album*, there are moments of light fillers, such as the excellently named The Dark Pages of Spring Give Lead to the New Leaves of Spring, or Black River, which are the album's Wild Honey Pie and Honey Pie, respectively. Why Walk When You Can Run is even similar in name to Why Don't We Just Do It in the Road?, although, it is another folky number.

Building from its pounding Noel Gallagher created drum loop, reminiscent of yet another Beatles' song, this time Tomorrow Never Knows, Echoes Round the Sun, is one of the album's less conventional tracks, and also another of its high-points. The driving intensity of the backing track, augmented by guitar licks and whirling Doors-esque string parts, creates a song about the biggest of all subjects, the universe: "On a rock, spinning through, the echoes round the sun", and shows just how ambitious Weller is with *22 Dreams*. The track's other-worldly-ness makes it an odd choice to accompany the more conventional Have You Made Up Your Mind as the album's first single, but it is this level of confidence in the maturity of his audience that is such a marked achievement on this album.

The last four or five tracks mark an end to matters, bringing the party to a careful conclusion with a run of piano and acoustic led ballads that are some of Weller's finniest. Whatever the feeling on the album, whether it be the conflicted feelings of love and loss on the title track, the mystical candour of Echoes Round the Sun, or the experimentation of 111 (the album's Revolution 9), Weller is clearly having a great time, because he is only too aware of what a good job he is doing.

The album finally comes around back on itself, with the aptly named Night Lights (the opening track is Light Nights), and we are offered a conclusion of sorts. Penultimate track Sea Spray is one of the best on the album, so it might seem strange having it buried right at the end (it was released as a single though), but its positioning urges listeners to make sure they take in every track. It reminds us that *22 Dreams* is nothing less of magnificent in its scale and grandeur. It is both intense and relaxed (One Bright Star is very laid back), and ranges from themes of life, death, love, freedom, loneliness, mortality, the universe, and everything in between.

Single 33:

All I Wanna Do (Is Be With You)/ Push It Along (Weller/Dine)
Released: 25th August 2008; UK Chart Position: 28; Label: Island; Album: *22 Dreams*
B-sides: Big Brass Buttons (Bobby Gillespie [Primal Scream remix])

UK Official Singles Chart – Top 10 – 31st August 2008:

1. I Kissed a Girl – Katy Perry
2. Pjando – Eric Prydz
3. Disturbia – Rhianna
4. The Man Who Can't Be Moved – The Script
5. Mountains – Biffy Clyro
6. All Summer Long – Kid Rock

7. Beggin' – Madcon
8. Dance Wiv Me – Dizzee Rascal/Harris/Chrome
9. Love is Noise – The Verve
10. 5 Years Time – Noah and the Whale

…………………………………………

28. All I Wanna Do (Is Be With You)/ Push It Along – Paul Weller

Sleek, capable pop acts like Katy Perry and Rhianna were proving that well made pop music was experiencing something of a renaissance as the noughties were drawing to a close, and it had only taken eight years to catch up. Rhianna was just 20 at the end of the summer in 2008, but she had already racked up 11 singles, two of which had reached number 1.

But then so too was indie-rock music having another go and being popular in 2008, with Biffy Clyro at number 5, their highest entry to date, whilst further down the chart The Verve were welcomed back with the excellent return to form track Love is Noise, while the Pavement-esque Noah and the Whale were down from 7 with their first top 10 single 5 Years Time.

<u>**Single 34:**</u>

Sea Spray (Weller/Andrews)/ 22 Dreams (Weller/Dine)
Released: 3rd November 2008; UK Chart Position: 59; Label: Island; Album: *22 Dreams*
B-sides: Have You Made Up Your Mind (acoustic)

UK Official Singles Chart – Top 10 – 9th November 2008:

1. Hero – X Factor Finalists
2. If I Were a Boy – Beyonce
3. The Promise – Girls Aloud
4. Womanizer – Britney Spears
5. Forgive Me – Leona Lewis
6. Infinity 2008 – Guru Josh Project
7. Hot n Cold – Katy Perry
8. The Boy Does Nothing – Alesha Dixon
9. Another Way to Die – Alicia Keys and Jack White
10. So What – Pink

....

59. Sea Spray/ 22 Dreams – Paul Weller

The less said about the pointless cover of Mariah Carey's Hero by that year's crop of *X Factor* finalists at number 1, the better, but aside from that, the run of solid pop tunes in the charts was continuing as 2008 drew to an end. Beyonce was at number 2 with her ode to sexual inequality, If I Were a Boy while Girls Aloud (granted, formed in a reality TV show) continued their run of interesting pop tracks; Britney was back with Womanizer; Leona Lewis (ok, another *X Factor* act...) was forging a great solo career; and Katy Perry, Alesha Dixon and Pink made up the list of seven female acts in the top 10.

Alicia Keys and Jack White's forgettable James Bond soundtrack song Another Way to Die, the theme song to the oddly named *Quantam of Solace* (Marc Webb, 2008) was at number 9, and way way down at 59 was Weller with the last single from *22 Dreams,* the excellent Sea Spray/ 22 Dreams.

Live Album 4:

Weller at the BBC
Released: 3rd November 2008; UK Chart Position: 32; Label: Island
Track Listing: CD1: Fly On The Wall (Johnnie Walker – Live, 05.09.1992); Pink On White Walls; Amongst Butterflies; Wild Wood (Saturday Sequence – Johnnie Walker, 02.10.1993); Hung Up; Out Of The Sinking; Clues; Whirlpools' End (Lunchtime Show – Emma Freud, 26.10.1994); Out Of The Sinking (acoustic) (Lunchtime Show, 01.11.1994); Broken Stones; Time Passes; The Changingman (Weller/Lynch); I Walk On Gilded Splinters (Creaux) [Evening Session, 08.05.1995]; Broken Stones (acoustic); You Do Something To Me (Simon Mayo, 12.09.1995); Brushed (Weller/Nelson/White); Peacock Suit; Up In Suze's Room; Friday Street; Mermaids; The Poacher (Lane) [Evening Session Live, 10.6.1997]
CD2: Driving Nowhere (Mark Goodier, 23.11.1997); Friday Street (acoustic) (BBC Radio 4 Kaleidoscope – Live In The Studio, 19.09.1997); Science (BBC Radio 1 Jo Wiley, 1997); Wishing On A Star; Thinking Of You (Edwards/Rodger) [BBC Radio 2 The Drivetime Show With Johnnie Walker, 01.09.2004]; Corrina, Corrina (David/Mahal); Early Morning Rain (Lightfoot); Foot Of The Mountain (Mark Lamarr For Jonathan Ross, 08.01.2005); To The Start Of Forever; Out Of The Sinking (BBC Radio 2 Janice Long, 04.03.2005); Paper Smile; Come On/Let's Go (The Drivetime Show With Stuart Maconie, 28.07.2005); Amongst Butterflies; Frightened; That's Entertainment (Mark Lamarr: Sold On Song, 11.02.2006); All I Wanna Do (Is Be With

You); Cold Moments; Push It Along (Dine/Weller); Pretty Flamingo (Barkan) [Mark Lamarr: God's Jukebox, 05.07.2008]
CD3: My Ever Changing Moods (Town and Country Club, 05.12.1990); A Man of Great Promise (Town and Country Club, 05.12.1990); Kosmos (Town and Country Club, 05.12.1990); Speak Like a Child (Town and Country Club, 05.12.1990); Just Like Yesterday (Town and Country Club, 05.12.1990); Work To Do (Isley/Isley/Isley) [Town and Country Club, 05.12.1990]; Pity Poor Alfie (Town and Country Club, 05.12.1990); What's Goin On (Cleveland/Gaye/Benson) [London Royal Albert Hall, 13.10.1992]; Uh Huh Oh Yeh! (Always There to Fool You!) [London Royal Albert Hall, 13.10.1992]; Hercules (Toussaint) [London Royal Albert Hall, 13.10.1992]; Bull-Rush/ Magic Bus (Townsend) [London Royal Albert Hall, 13.10.1992]; Above The Clouds (London Royal Albert Hall, 13.10.1992); Everything Has A Price To Pay (London Royal Albert Hall, 13.10.1992); Headstart For Happiness (London Royal Albert Hall, 13.10.1992); Into Tomorrow (London Royal Albert Hall, 13.10.1992); Porcelain Gods (Phoenix Festival, 13.07.1995); Stanley Road (Phoenix Festival, 13.07.1995); Can You Heal Us (Holy Man) [Phoenix Festival, 13.07.1995]
CD4: Shadow Of The Sun (Phoenix Festival, 13.07.1995); I Walk On Gilded Splinters (Creaux) (w. Noel Gallagher) [Phoenix Festival, 13.07.1995]; Out Of The Sinking (Finsbury Park, 09.06.1996); Hung Up (Finsbury Park, 09.06.1996); Sunflower (Finsbury Park, 09.06.1996); Broken Stones (Finsbury Park, 09.06.1996); Fly On The Wall (Finsbury Park,

09.06.1996); Tales From the Riverbank (Finsbury Park, 09.06.1996); Peacock Suit (London Victoria Park, 08.08.1998); Heavy Soul (London Victoria Park, 08.08.1998); Science (London Victoria Park, 08.08.1998); I Didn't Mean To Hurt You (BBC Radio Theatre, 09.11.1998); Brand New Start (BBC Radio Theatre, 09.11.1998); Wild Wood (BBC Radio Theatre, 09.11.1998); Friday Street (BBC Radio Theatre, 09.11.1998); The Changingman (Weller/Lynch) [BBC Radio Theatre 09.11.1998]
Producer/s: various BBC producers

UK Official Albums Chart – Top 10 – 9th November 2008:

1. *Out of Control* – Girls Aloud
2. *Funhouse* – Pink
3. *Greatest Hits* – Enrique Iglesias
4. *Slipway Fires* – Razorlight
5. *A Hundred Million Suns* – Snow Patrol
6. *Only by the Night* – Kings of Leon
7. *My Love – The Essential Collection* – Celine Dion
8. *Pictures – 40 Years of Hits* – Status Quo
9. *Black Ice* – AC/DC
10. *The Best Of* – Sash

....

32. *Weller at the BBC – Paul Weller*

There is no real surprise that the mega four CD, or even the two CD (or the 13 CD's worth of download), versions of *Weller at the BBC* didn't chart higher than 32. A collection like that is only really for the uber fans, plus, by 2008, Spotify was beginning to find its feet (est. April 2006), and fans could look up nearly anything an artist had done for a small monthly charge. The compilation was really for completists, and it did incredibly well sales-wise considering.

Weller at the BBC

Released the same day as the last single from *22 Dreams*, Sea Spray/ 22 Dreams, *Weller at the BBC* was a mammoth boxed set of all of Weller's recordings at, you guessed it, the BBC. It was released as a four CD boxed set, a two CD highlights package, and the mega, download only, 13 CD's worth boxed set (download only) for the real obsessive.

The four CD boxed set, which is included here for reasons of brevity, was divided into two halves, the sessions, so the versions of songs that Weller recorded for TV and radio, including Johnnie Walker's Radio 2 *Saturday Sequence*, plus Emma Freud's lunchtime show, shows hosted by Simon Mayo, Mark Lamarr, as well as the legendary *Evening Sessions*, from the mid and late nineties.

The second half is made up of live performances from the Royal Albert Hall in 1992, the Phoenix Festival from 1995, plus massive concerts at Finsbury and Victoria Park, all captured by the BBC and either aired at the time or saved for later.

As part of the major Weller retrospective that his fiftieth year on the planet was shaping up to be, there couldn't really be much of a better of celebrating his 16 years as a solo artist (31 years as a recording artist) than a major collection of Weller doing what he does best – playing live – in a major range of settings, including the intimacy of an *Evening Session* studio, the vast indoor space of the Royal Albert Hall, and the massive outdoor space of various festivals. Similarly, the vast range of solo tracks on offer here means that there is something for everyone, with The

Changingman set amongst The Poacher (the Small Faces track) and even That's Entertainment, and The Who's Magic Bus.

Time to Wake Up, Again

Weller was away touring around the UK for much of 2009, finally entering the studio to record a new album after a couple of summer festival dates in Spain, as well as the world-famous Fuji Rock Festival in Japan. Black Barn Studios was once again the location for recording the new set of songs, and Weller's plan with the new album was to shake things up once more.

Now old hand Simon Dine was back at the mixing desk, and the album was given the provocative title of *Wake Up the Nation*. It found its way to number 2 in the charts in April 2010, and was preceded by Paul's last single to reach the top 40, another double A-side, No Tears to Cry/ Wake Up the Nation, released 12th April.

7&3 Is the Strikers Name, was released as a single back in December 2009 as limited edition 7" only, and so didn't chart.

For the first time, Simon Dine was given co-writing credits on all of the 16 tracks on the album.

Single 35:

No Tears to Cry/ Wake Up the Nation
Released: 12th April 2010; UK Chart Position: 26;
Label: Island; Album: *Wake Up the Nation*
B-sides: Mistress Brown

(all tracks written by Weller/Dine)

UK Official Singles Chart – Top 10 – 26th April 2010:

1. OMG – Usher ft. Will I Am
2. This Ain't a Love Song – Scouting for Girls
3. I Need you Tonight – Professor Green ft. Ed Drewett
4. She Said – Plan B
5. Acapella – Kelis
6. Telephone – Lady Gaga ft. Beyonce
7. Naturally – Selena Gomez and The Scene
8. Carry Out – Timbaland ft. Justin Timberlake
9. Pass Out – Tinie Tempah
10. Hot – Inna

....

26. No Tears to Cry/ Wake Up the Nation – Paul Weller

With physical sales making up a very small minority of chart positioning (although physical copies did still need to be available), and streaming still four years away from being counted, the singles chart in 2010 consisted mainly of tracks downloaded for £0.99 (or lower) from iTunes, or similar. This means that certain music was much more prominent than others, and the likes of Beyonce, Timbaland and Lady Gaga ruled the roost.

Weller could not have been more removed from the top 10 in April 2010 than at any point in his career, and it is a testament to two great A-sides that he made it into the top 30 at all. Sadly, this single was Weller's last to reach the top 30, to date.

Album 10:

Wake Up the Nation
Released: 19th April 2010; UK Chart Position: 2; Label: Island
Track Listing: Moonshine; Wake Up the Nation; No Tears to Cry; Fast Car/ Slow Traffic; Andromeda; In Amsterdam; She Speaks; Find the Torch, Burn the Plans; Aim High; Trees; Grasp & Still Connect; Whatever Next; 7&3 Is the Strikers Name; Up the Dosage; Pieces of Dream; Two Fat Ladies
Producer: Simon Dine

(all tracks written by Weller/Dine)

UK Official Albums Chart – Top 10 – 25th April 2010:

1. *Iron Man 2 – OST* – AC/DC
2. ***Wake Up the Nation* – Paul Weller**
3. *The Defamation of Strickland Banks* – Plan B
4. *Hang Cool Teddy Bear* – Meat Loaf
5. *Everybody Wants to be On TV* – Scouting for Girls
6. *The Fame* – Lady Gaga
7. *Sunny Side Up* – Paolo Nutini
8. *My Best Friend is You* – Kate Nash
9. *My World* – Justin Bieber
10. *Lungs* – Florence & the Machine

AC/DC's official soundtrack to *Iron Man 2* (Favreau, 2010) at number 1 ahead of *Wake Up the Nation*, says more about the growing success of the Marvel franchise than it does about the quality of Weller's new record.

Behind Weller, the excellent *The Defamation of Strickland Banks* by rapper Plan B was at number 3, down from a deserved number 1. The album, just his second, manages to reinvent UK hip-hop music, and gave a new lease of life to the concept album at the same time. Aside from that, Lady Gaga continued to reinvent art and pop, whilst Florence & the Machine's excellent second album, *Lungs*, props up the top 10, down from a deserved number 1.

Wake Up the Nation

His first album to be nominated for the Mercury Music Prize since *Wild Wood* back in 1993, says something about how current Weller was finding himself as the second decade of the new millennium began, and he entered his fourth decade as a recording artist. That year's Mercury went to minimalist rockers The xx and their self-named debut album, but the short list was jam-packed with an eclectic mix of rock, pop, hip-hop and folk, notably Foals' *Total Life Forever*, former winner Dizzee Rascal's *Tongue n' Cheek*, Laura Marling's *I Speak Because I Can*, and Wild Beasts' *Two Dancers*. The most experienced artist by some way, Weller's tenth studio album was in some great company, and it stood up.

Finding himself promoted not only to co-songwriter on every track, but also to key producer, Simon Dine's role in Weller's band had steadily grown over the years, and *Wake Up the Nation* was his first proper opportunity to exert a bigger level of influence. It was Dine's idea to produce a record that was "urban, tough and quite metallic"[xxxiv]. Opening track Moonshine appearing as just this. It's a frantic yet tuneful piece of punk rock, in debt to I Wanna Be

Your Dog by The Stooges, and starts off the album like so many of its predecessors, with a slice of proper rock 'n' roll.

Although song writing credits were limited to just Weller and Dine, the guest slots were just as plentiful as *22 Dreams* (not surprising considering the album has 16 tracks, not far off a double itself), and there are a couple of surprises. With Steve White gone, it is Bev Bevan, the legendary drummer for ELO and Black Sabbath (amongst others), who plays on the opening two tracks, providing that much needed back beat to get the album moving.

Bruce Foxton also returns to play his Rickenbacker bass on Fast Car/ Slow Traffic and She Speaks, for the first time since The Jam disbanded back in 1982. Paul, having recently lost his father, mentor and manager John, reached out to Foxton when he lost his wife Pat around the same time, and the pair even played together live at the *Wake Up Woking* fundraiser event in July 2010, harmonising like they used to on the old Jam tracks the Butterfly Collector, sparking unfounded rumours of a Jam reunion.

Guest spots and producer credits aside, there is no doubt just whose album *Wake Up the Nation* is though, and Weller's song writing, guitar playing, and guttural vocal delivery are more refined with every passing note. The lead single Wake Up the Nation is classic Weller, in the same vein as From the Floorboards Up (with added flute), No Tears to Cry changes the tempo and adds in the acoustic and another big chorus (and wouldn't have sounded out of place on a sixties Motown album), whilst Fast Car/ Slow Traffic takes Weller (and Foxton) back to 1978 *All Mod Cons* era Jam, complete with Foxton's prominent rolling bass line and harmony backing vocals.

Sixteen tracks may seem like another daunting prospect for a Weller album, but with four of them less than two minutes in length, plus the odd instrumental, the result is an album that jogs along at a hectic pace, leaping from track to track before the listener has a chance of getting bored. The most unexpected guest spot is perhaps Kevin Shields, the legendary perfectionist from noise-smiths My Bloody Valentine, who famously near-bankrupt Creation Records with the recording of band's third album back in the early nineties. Alongside Weller and Foxton, Shields' guitar supplements the low-key track perfectly, and he was even asked back to play on track 13, 7&3 Is the Strikers Name.

Find the Torch/ Burn the Plans is the album's centre point and one of the biggest tracks, and uses The Woking Gay Community Choir to great effect on backing vocals. The track would also give its name to Weller's next live album, recorded at his favourite venue, the Royal Albert Hall.

Although no less ambitious in scope than *22 Dreams*, *Wake Up the Nation* lacks its predecessor's eclecticism. A move made on purpose in order to deliver on that tough urban image, and to try and draw in the corners of the record to deliver something more concrete and more recognisable as a Weller solo record. Like *22 Dreams*, *Wake Up the Nation* went gold just a week after its release[xxxv], meaning it sold 100k physical units, in a time when people were buying fewer and fewer records. This, combined with the Mercury nomination, helped Weller to understand that he was still on the right track. Not only his many many fans, but also the music bods who decide what is and what isn't good music, were interested in him, and for a man not a million years away from getting his free bus pass, this must have been the most fulfilling feeling yet.

Despite its seemingly cumbersome 16 tracks, *Wake Up the Nation* was one of Weller's tightest solo records to date, and set him and his recording career on the trajectory, an album focused one that leaves the singles chart behind, that he is still on today.

Single 36:

Find the Torch, Burn the Plans
Released: 14th June 2010; UK Chart Position: 68;
Label: Island; Album: *Wake Up the Nation*
B-sides: All I Wanna Do (Is Be With You) [acoustic, recorded "Wiener Blut" Berlin by RBB Radioeins]; Moonshine (recorded live from the BBC Theatre)

(all tracks written by Weller/Dine)

UK Official Singles Chart – Top 10 – 20th June 2010:

1. Shout – Shout ft. Dizzee and James Corden
2. Wavin' Flag – K'Naan
3. Kickstarts – Example
4. All the Lovers – Kylie Minogue
5. Frisky – Tinie Tempah ft. Labrinth
6. Not Afraid – Eminem
7. Gettin' Over – David Guetta ft. Chris Willis
8. Dancing on My Own – Robyn
9. Ridin' Solo – Jason Derulo
10. Alejandro – Lady Gaga

....

68. Find the Torch, Burn the Plans – Paul Weller

CHAPTER EIGHT
Find The Torch, Burn The Plans – Live at The Royal Albert Hall, Sonik Kicks and *More Modern Classics* (2011-2014)

By 2010 the charts and how people engaged with music was changing, more than at any time in its 60-year history. With physical sales of singles (and albums) at their lowest in 2004 and downloaded music on the increase in the same period, downloads were incorporated into the main chart in April 2005.

However, with the online streaming services like *Spotify* becoming more popular than downloads in the same period, space also had to be made for subscription services to be incorporated if the charts were going to be truly representative of popular music and what people were really listening to.

It took nearly ten years for this to take effect, and it was July 2014 before streaming was finally incorporated into the main charts. For an artist like Paul Weller, who was used to releasing three or four singles to help promote an album, this meant huge changes were afoot. Weller's audience is loyal, but they are an albums audience, and unlikely to buy singles other than to get their hands on B-sides, which as we have come to see, are often made available on collections anyway.

This is why none of the 18 singles – or 'impact tracks' as they are now known – Weller has released since 2014 have charted, and as such, this is why none of them are featured in the rest of this book. For reasons of brevity, I have also only included the ones that charted in the top 100 between 2010 and 2014, and none of the limited-edition ones.

Weller has often spoken out about his dislike of *Spotify*. His main bone of contention being that the artist receives such a pittance from streams of their songs. As of 2019 it is estimated that "*Spotify* pays less than a cent: about $0.003 to $0.0084 per stream"[xxxvi]. Weller's biggest streamed song is You Do Something to Me, for which he would have received approx. $136k (£102k) for 34million streams.

Although, it is the smaller artists that he is piping up for. Newer bands like The Mysterines, whose lead singer Lea Metcalfe would appear on *Fat Pop*, and whose top 5 songs have been streamed 6.4million times on *Spotify*. Meaning they would (presumably) each have a quarter share in $25.6k (£19.2k). I guess it's better than working in *Burger King*.

In April 2021, an open letter signed by 156 musicians – led by Sir Paul McCartney and Kate Bush – was sent to British PM Boris Johnson asking for the 1988 Copyright Act to be reworded "to bring royalty payments more in line with how those in radio are paid, while acknowledging the very different on-demand nature of streaming"[xxxvii], to try and ensure that artists are no longer exploited. No word from Bojo (he's got too much on his hands with COVID, perhaps), but a court case in the USA in 2017 ruled that the streaming services should raise the level of royalties they pay musicians. Spotify, Google, Amazon and Pandora appealed and the "companies scored a partial win in August 2020, with a court finding fault in the methodology used to calculate the new rates, requiring them to be recalculated"[xxxviii]. The case is yet to be resolved.

The counter argument is that bands, and Weller too, would never receive as much attention were their music not available on *Spotify* for people to access so easily. And a quarter share of something is better than Sean Parker's quarter share of nothing model back in the days of *Napster*. And this is of course true, as long as bands have other revenue streams. Like playing live. Well, guess what happened in 2020.

Perhaps bands should be grateful that they are making anything from playing music. Now considered one of the most important bands of their era, Joy Division all had day jobs until they were forced to give them up when their schedule became too gruelling. It was only really in the mid-nineties that indie bands like Oasis began to make a lot of money, before then groups were happy to just get by. The egalitarianism of *Spotify* is not only bringing order back to the charts, but also returning indie music to the era of the struggling artist. Perhaps that's what is needed in order for Britain to produce another Joy Division.

Doubling Down

Weller's way of reacting to the changing times was to double down on his own mystique by varying his release schedule, and over the next few years he put many limited-edition singles. Starlite was released in August 2011 as a stand-alone single, and despite being limited to 3000 copies, still made 113 in the charts. Flame-Out/ The Olde Original, which was included on the best-of *More Modern Classics*, was released on 7" vinyl only, in support of Record Store Day in 2013.

A large quantity of the singles were bought up by touts and stuck on eBay, changing hands for much more than they were originally sold for, drawing much ire from fans and from Weller himself. Despite this, the single still made 132 in the charts. In 2014 he released Brand New Toy (again for Record Store Day), and also included on *More Modern Classics*, this time, ensuring the right processes were put in place to make sure the touts couldn't get their hands on them.

Also released between 2011 and 2012 were Around the Lake (his 36th single) and The Attic (his 39th single). Both tracks were taken from *Sonik Kicks* and were not limited (so are included in the overall singles count here), but both were released as download only. Neither managed to chart, showing us that, at this point at least, Weller's fanbase still preferred the physical copies of his singles.

However, as much as music changes, it also manages to stay the same, and Weller's prolificacy has only increased as his popularity has. Of the five studio albums he released between 2015 and 2021, all have all charted in the top 5. This means he is just as valid and current as he has ever been, and the charts are being properly representational by capturing what (and how) people are listening to music.

Another Collectors' Edition

Back in May 2008 Weller released on CD *Live at the Royal Albert Hall*. It was the audio accompaniment to the DVD of the same concert, released back in November 2000, not long after the concert date it captured. Because that live album failed to chart in the top 100 (despite eventually going gold), and because Weller also released another major collectors' edition DVD and CD, also of a concert at the Royal Albert Hall, in November 2010, it is the latter that is included here.

Live Album 4:

Find the Torch, Burn the Plans – Live at the Royal Albert Hall
Released: 29th November 2010; UK Chart Position: 72; Label: Island
Track Listing: CD1: Andromeda (Weller/Dine); From the Floorboards Up; 7&3 Is A Strikers Name (Weller/Dine); Into Tomorrow; Aim High (Weller/Dine); Moonshine; Up the Dosage; Trees (Weller/Dine); Wild Wood; The Eton Rifled (ft. Kelly Jones); That's Entertainment (ft. Kelly Jones); Fast Car/ Slow Traffic (Weller/Dine)
CD2: (In Concert at the BBC Theatre) Start!; Sea Spray (Weller/Anderson); Strange Town; Broken Stones; How Sweet It Is (To Be Loved By You) (ft. Lauren Pritchard) [Holland/Dozier/Holland]; No Tears to Cry (ft. Richard Hawley) [Weller/Dine]
Producer/s: various

UK Official Albums Chart – Top 10 – 5th December 2010:

1. *Progress* – Take That
2. *Olly Murs* – Olly Murs
3. *Outta This World* – JLS
4. *Loud* – Rihanna
5. *The Gift* – Susan Boyle
6. *Greatest Hits* – Bon Jovi
7. *Love Live Life* – N-Dubz
8. *Crazy Love* – Michael Buble
9. *Endlessly* – Duffy
10. *Moonlight Serenade* – Andre Rieu & Johann Strauss

....

72. *Find the Torch, Burn the Plans* – Paul Weller

Take That's third album since their much publicised reformation *Progress* was at the top spot in December 2010, but the key thing that can be garnered from the top 10 albums at the beginning of the second decade of the new millennium, was the continuing dominance of the reality shows on the charts. Gary Barlow (the formerly fat one who writes the songs for Take That) and Tulisa from N-Dubz (no. 7 with *Love Live Life*) were both judges on the *X-Factor* between 2011 and 2012, and Olly Murs, JLS and Susan Boyle all came to fame via *X-Factor* and *Britain's Got Talent.*

Interestingly, none of the biggest artists to gain longevity won the *X-Factor*, both Olly Murs and JLS came in second, and the biggest act to emerge from the show by quite some way, One Direction, came in third place, behind Rebecca Ferguson and Matt Cardle, both of whom disappeared not long after the show. As for Susan Boyle, she was also the runner up of her season of *Britain's Got Talent*, coming in second to dance group Diversity in 2009, and she has gone on to become one of the biggest reality stars the country has ever produced. Her first three albums all reached number 1, and by 2019, she had released seven albums in total.

Back on the Road

Weller, meanwhile, continued to tour throughout most of the second half of 2010, first into Europe, the Netherlands, Belgium, Germany and France, before a five night residency at the Royal Albert Hall from 24th-28th May (from which the *Find the Torch...* recordings were taken), and back around the UK, Ireland, Spain, Italy, France, Norway, Sweden, and the UK summer festivals, even stopping in at the Jersey

Live Festival in September. Then on to Australia for October, the USA in November, and back to the UK for end of November, and December, finishing up at Wembley Arena on 10th December.

In April 2011 Weller was supported at the Brixton Academy by the newly formed Beady Eye, the band that grew from the ashes of Oasis, featuring the entire line up minus Noel Gallagher (Liam, Gem Archer, Andy Bell and Chris Sharrock), and who had played just a handful of gigs before Weller offered them a support slot. And on 22nd and 23rd June, Weller played two massive shows in Hyde Park. There was no doubting that he continued to be at the very top of his game.

Throughout 2010 and 2011 though, Weller was still tinkering around in Black Barn Studios with new material, and the result was a new album, *Sonik Kicks*, released in March 2012, going straight in at number 1 in the albums chart. The first single from the album, That Dangerous Age, was released a week earlier, on 12th March 2012.

Single 39:

That Dangerous Age (Weller/Dine)
Released: 12th March 2012; UK Chart Position: 66;
Label: Island; Album: *Sonik Kicks*
B-sides: Portal to the Past; That Dangerous Age (Ladytron remix) [Weller/Dine]

UK Official Singles Chart – Top 10 – 18th March 2012:

1. Somebody That I Used to Know – Gotye ft. Kimbra
2. Starships – Nicki Minaj

3. Elephant – Alexandra Burke/ Erick Morillo
4. Next to Me – Emeli Sande
5. Wild Ones – Flo Rida ft. Sia
6. Titanium – David Guetta ft. Sia
7. Hot Right Now – DJ Fresh ft. Rita Ora
8. Turn Me On – David Guetta ft. Nicki Minaj
9. Love Me – Stooshe ft. Travis McCoy
10. N***s in Paris – Jay-Z & Kanye West

....

66. That Dangerous Age – Paul Weller

The ten songs in the mid-March 2012 top 10 seemed to feature the same four or five artists arranged in a slightly different order. French DJ David Guetta features twice, as does mysterious Australian singer Sia, and rapper Nicki Minaj.

Rap heavyweights Jay-Z and Kanye West have teamed up on the highly censored N***s in Paris, and the music is so far removed from what Weller was up to at the time, it was probably for the best that he found his single limping to number 66.

Album 11:

Sonik Kicks
Released: 19th March 2012; UK Chart Position: 1; Label: Island
Track Listing: Green; The Attic; Kling I Klang; Sleep of the Serene (Weller/Ibrahim/Rees); By the Waters (Weller/Ibrahim); That Dangerous Age; Study in Blue; Dragonfly (P. Weller/J. Weller/Dine); When Your Garden's Overgrown; Around the Lake; Twilight (Weller/Cradock); Drifters (Weller/Cradock/Dine); Paperchase; Be Happy Children

Producer/s: Paul Weller; Simon Dine

(all songs written by Weller/Dine, unless otherwise indicated)

UK Official Albums Chart – Top 10 – 25th March 2012:

1. ***Sonik Kicks* – Paul Weller**
2. *Nothing but the Beat* – David Guetta
3. *In My Dreams* – Military Wives
4. *Our Version Events* – Emeli Sande
5. *21* – Adele
6. *Born to Dire* – Lana Del Rey
7. *Mylo Xyloto* – Coldplay
8. + – Ed Sheeran
9. *Wrecking Ball* – Bruce Springsteen
10. *Home Again* – Michael Kiwanuka

At total odds with the singles chart in the same period, there were some real heavy hitters in the top 10 in March 2012 when Weller claimed his fourth solo number 1 album. Bruce Springsteen, the Boss himself, has more longevity than Weller (just about, *Born to Run* was released in 1975); Coldplay's fifth album *Mylo Xyloto* was also their fifth to reach number 1; and Ed Sheeran's debut album + had already been in the UK Albums Chart since September 2011 (and had been number 1 on three separate occasions).

But it was Adele's second album *21* that really took home the plaudits (and still does). By March 2012 it had been in the top 10 for 60 weeks, and had already beaten Oasis' *(What's the Story) Morning Glory?* to become the second highest selling UK studio album of all time (behind The Beatles' *Sgt. Pepper...*), despite being released in a time when people apparently didn't buy records. *21*'s initial run at the top spot had been 11 weeks, and at time of writing it is back up at number 13[xxxix].

So, Island timed the release of Weller's new album perfectly, and he found his way onto the top of a pile of very high achievers, proving that whatever happened in the singles chart, Weller was still king of the album. By July 2012, *Sonik Kicks* album had gone silver, meaning it had sold in excess of 60k units[xl], continuing his run at the top.

Sonik Kicks

Weller's last album for Island was also his last new album for three years. It was his eleventh studio album and appeared in his twentieth year as a solo artist, meaning that on average he had released more than one album every two years by this point.

The album finds Weller at a pretty stable position in his life. About to turn 54, he was married to singer Hannah Anderson, who had given birth to twin boys (Bowie and John Paul) two weeks before *Sonik Kicks* was released. He also had a great relationship with his other kids. Natt had joined him on stage playing guitar, and Jessie was given co-writing credit for writing the lyrics to track 8 on *Sonik Kicks*, Dragonfly. Also playing on that song were both Noel Gallagher (who plays bass), and Graham Coxon (Hammond organ), making the song something of a Britpop reunion, of sorts, Weller playing a part at ending the famous Oasis/Blur feud for good.

With all this familial bliss surrounding him, you might expect *Sonik Kicks* to kick about as much weight as a wet tea towel, but with age, not only has

Weller gained happiness, but also experience, and opening track Green shares more in common with dance acts like Death in Vegas, *Xtrmntr* era Primal Scream, or New Order on amphetamines, than it does the Small Faces. Whilst the second track, the third and final single, The Attic, finds the band back on more familiar ground, a driving rhythm augmented by sultry strings.

Kling I Klang (a reference to German electro-pioneers Kraftwerk) fades into the instrumental and experimental Sleep of the Serene, penned by Aziz Ibrahim (he of the God voice), which in turn transforms into the beautiful acoustic strum of By the Waters (also played by Ibrahim), without a break in the music, creating a ten minute long piece of music that is up there with the best stuff that Weller has ever done. The latter title is one of the strongest tracks on the album, and alongside Weller, and Ibrahim's guitar, there are just some delicate strings to help showcase the sonorous track.

First single proper from the album, That Dangerous Age, is another upbeat number, easy to listen to on the radio, but seemingly about a man (and later a woman) going through a mid-life crisis ("he likes three sugars in his coffee, he's at that dangerous age, he wants that chick in the office"). The song's little domestic story positions itself as *All Mod Cons*-era Jam, now all grown up. Or in an act of master copying disciple, like a track from Blur's *Parklife*.

Jude Rogers, who reviewed the album for the BBC, wasn't wrong when she described it as "An emotional, experimental ride"[xli], and the tracks, layered with the typical drum, bass, keys and riff laden guitar tracks, leap from one to the next like they're in a rush to find out what the next song is going to be. Most of the tracks barely last longer than three minutes, the epic extended jam of Study in Blue, and Paperchase, notable exceptions. The album was dedicated to Amy Winehouse, who had died suddenly in August 2011, and who Weller had worked with, performing an emotional version of Etta James' Don't Got to Strangers on *Later... with Jules Holland*, back in 2006. Paperchase is clearly about Winehouse, and the tragic loss of her incredible talent, with Weller singing:

Paper planes - paper planes
Flying too close to the solar flames
Paper chains - paper chains
Was earth not enough for you?

Dragonfly, the Britpop all-starer track, consists of a Mani-in-Primal-Scream style bass (played by Noel G.), a sound not used much in Weller's music, and the track is the group's best go at Scream-like psychedelia, and a solid centrepiece for an experimental Weller album. The brilliantly named When Your Garden's Overgrown is classic Weller, all strummed major chords and layered harmony lines, and Around the Lake continues to use that same ominous Mani-esque bass line. The final track is a gentle ode to love and life, summed up perfectly by its title, Be Happy Children, awash with those same computer bleeps, so prominent on the album.

As Weller had learnt to do on his previous two albums, *Sonik Kicks* succeeds because he opens up his song writing shop to outside influence, and most notably on this album, to musical experimentation. There isn't one track that goes by without some form of keyboard programming, drum loop, or left field percussion instrument (what exactly is a celeste?), to help build the basic band tracks, which are just as faithful to Weller's well-known sound as ever.

Single 40:
Birthday (Lennon/McCartney) Released: 18th June 2012 (one day only); UK Chart Position: 64; Label: Island; Album: n/a B-sides: n/a

UK Official Singles Chart – Top 10 – 24th June 2012:

1. Payphone – Maroon 5 ft. Wiz Khalifa
2. Call My Name – Cheryl
3. Whistle – Flo Rida
4. Black Heart – Stooshe
5. Princess of China – Coldplay and Rihanna
6. Feel the Love – Rudimental ft. John Newman
7. We Are Young – Fun ft. Janelle Monae
8. Call Me Maybe – Carly Rae Jepsen
9. Scream – Usher
10. Picking up the Pieces – Paloma Faith

....

64. Birthday – Paul Weller

Recorded in honour of Paul McCartney's 70th birthday, Weller released his version of The Beatles' song Birthday (from *The White Album*) on download only, making it available for just one day. Despite this super limited edition (sort of, being a download, it was completely unlimited quantity-wise), the single still managed to reach number 64 in the charts, the last of Weller's singles to make the top 100.

More Modern Classics

And then that was it from Weller for a while. Aside from joining Damon Albarn and Noel Gallagher playing drums live on Blur's Tender in March 2013. He released the Flame-Out!/ The olde Original single on 7" vinyl only on 20th April, 2013, Record Store Day, and appeared live at Rough Trade in East London in honour of the event, but there was no new music until *Saturns Pattern* in May 2015. There were lots of live appearances throughout the summer of 2013 though, including Hard Rock Calling at Olympia Park, Kew Gardens and Edinburgh Castle, as well as a tour of the USA and another of the UK in late 2013.

Then in June 2014 came yet another best-of, but one that this time focused on all of the solo albums he had released since *Heliocentric*. It was released in three separate editions, including the 1-disc CD, the vinyl edition, and the full 3-disc CD collection, and it reached number 6 in the UK Albums Chart.

Best of Album no. 3:

More Modern Classics
Released: 2nd June 2014; UK Chart Position: 6; Label: Virgin/EMI
Track Listing: He's the Keeper; Sweet Pea, My Sweet Pea; It's Written in the Stars*; Wishing on a Star (Calvin); From the Floorboards Up; Come On/ Let's Go; Wild Blue Yonder; Have You Made Up Your Mind; Echoes Round the Sun (Weller/Gallagher); All I Wanna Do (Is Be With You); Push It Along*; 22 Dreams*; No Tears to Cry*; Wake Up the Nation*; Fast Car/ Slow Traffic*; Starlite*; That Dangerous Age*; When

Your Garden's Overgrown*; The Attic*; Flame-Out; Brand New Toy
Producer/s: Paul Weller; Brendon Lynch; Simon Dine; Jan Kybert; Charles Rees

*written by Weller/Dine

UK Official Albums Chart – Top 10 – 8th June 2014:

1. *In the Lonely Hour* – Sam Smith
2. *Ghost Stories* – Coldplay
3. *New Eyes* – Clean Bandit
4. *Caustic Love* – Paulo Nutini
5. *A Perfect Contradiction* – Paloma Faith
6. ***More Modern Classics* – Paul Weller**
7. *Led Zeppelin* – Led Zeppelin
8. *Hank* – Hank Marvin
9. *Xscape* – Michael Jackson
10. *Led Zeppelin III* – Led Zeppelin

With streaming now counting toward chart positions, popular music was becoming more divisive than ever. Some acts – Coldplay, Ed Sheeran, Sam Smith – managed to straddle both the singles and the albums chart, staying on trend, and defining the corners of popular music. Yet other acts, like Paul Weller, found themselves moving away from impacting upon the singles chart, and taking up residency in the albums chart.

For an album to count toward the main chart, at least six tracks from that album need to be streamed (with a maximum of 12), so individual songs picked off and added to playlists, will only contribute toward the singles chart. One thousand album streams are then counted as one album sale.

So, in 2014, the albums chart became the residency of the more serious artist, and fell in line with the overall democratisation of the charts. No longer did record companies need to actually release music for it to sell, although they still did of course, but if enough people happened to stream *Led Zeppelin* (or *Led Zeppelin III*), then that album would find its way back into the charts, with little or no influence from marketing forces. In many ways, the charts post-2014, helped cut out the middleman, and Hank Marvin found himself sat alongside Paloma Faith, Clean Bandit, and the second posthumous album by Michael Jackson, *Xscape*. It was a whole new world.

CHAPTER NINE

The Parlophone Years – *Saturns Pattern, A Kind Revolution, True Meanings* and *Other Aspects – Live at the Royal Festival Hall (2015-2019)*

As well as three new albums between 2015 and 2019, in 2017, Weller also contributed the soundtrack to the British boxing film *Jawbone* (Napper, 2017), written by and starring Johnny Harris (from *This is England '86* [Meadows, 2010]), and featuring Ray Winstone, Ian McShane and Michael Smiley.

Amazingly, *Jawbone* was the first soundtrack Weller had been so directly involved with, and he is credited as both writer and producer of the seven-track mini-album. He threw himself into the project as he does all of his albums, sending Harris samples of tracks he had written, which in turn inspired the re-writes of the script. Sober for nearly seven years by 2017, it was perhaps the story of an alcoholic trying to turn his life around through channelling his energy into boxing that caught Weller's eye.

The track The Ballad of Jimmy McCabe, is a particularly heart-felt folky song played on just an acoustic and helps bring some shape and colour to what could otherwise have been a fairly typical rags-to-riches sports film. Inspired by Harris' work with Shane Meadows, the song has the feel of one of the jangly folk tracks that the Uttoxeter auteur often uses in his films, particularly in the twisted story of revenge that in part inspired *Jawbone*, 2004's *Dead Man's Shoes*.

Back to the Studio

Preceded by the single of the same name, which was released on 7" and 12" vinyl and download only, on 11th May 2015, *Saturns Pattern* was Weller's twelve studio album, released a week later than the single, on 18th May.

Album 12:
Saturns Pattern Released: 18th May 2015; UK Chart Position: 2; Label: Parlophone Track Listing: White Sky; Saturns Pattern; Going My Way; Long Time; Pick It Up; I'm Where I Should Be; Phoenix; In the Car...; These City Streets Producer/s: Paul Weller; Jan Kybert
(all songs written by Weller/Kybert)

UK Official Albums Chart – Top 10 – 24th May 2015:

1. *The Desired Effect* – Brandon Flowers
2. ***Saturns Pattern* – Paul Weller**
3. *Wilder Mind* – Mumford & Sons
4. *1989* – Taylor Swift
5. *In the Lonely Hour* – Sam Smith
6. *Sol Invictus* – Faith No More
7. *Hozier* – Hozier
8. *Number 1 to Infinity* – Mariah Carey
9. *X* – Ed Sheeran
10. *The Ultimate Collection* – Paul Simon

Heading straight into the chart one place behind Killers front man Brandon Flowers' solo album, *The Desired Effect*, the grammatically questionable *Saturns Pattern* peaked at number 2 in the UK Albums Chart in May 2015, the day before Weller turned 57. The new chart working in Weller's favour, the album spent nine weeks in the top 100, where *Sonik Kicks* had hung around for just five.

Alongside Weller was the usual mix of new artists – Taylor Swift, Sam Smith and the omnipresent Ed Sheeran – and more established artists such as Mumford & Sons, American rockers Faith No More, and a new Paul Simon best-of. It was good company for Weller to keep, the post-2014 charts having levelled out the type of albums that were proving the most popular.

Saturns Pattern

The Weller album with the fewest tracks (just nine), *Saturns Pattern* though is not his shortest (that accolade goes to the first Jam album, *In the City* at 32 mins and 2 seconds). Rather, it is the album on which Weller has chosen to explore fewer songs, but in more detail, running times often reaching the four minutes and beyond mark. Epics like Pick it Up (6 mins, 16 seconds) and the excellent Phoenix (dedicated to the house DJ Frankie Knuckles), run much longer than you would usually expect, just because they can, and the Modfather is clearly having such a good time playing them.

It is also the album in which fans and critics considered he 'returned to his roots', Paul Moody in *Classic Rock* saying:

Long term fans will breathe a sigh of relief that The Modfather is finally back on familiar turf... Weller has spoken recently about his desire to restore some 'soul' to his music and Saturns Pattern *signals a reconnection to both his own (and his audiences') core musical values*[xlii]*.*

That 'soul' however appears in a purely Weller way. It is evident in the intro and piano line to In the Car..., and the feel of Phoenix, but opening track White Sky ignites the album in the way that only an opening Weller number can. Backwards guitars emerge from vast emptiness, soon giving way to a fat distorted guitar riff, soon joined by huge drums, distorted vocals and layer upon layer of programming, presenting an opening track that is one of his best rock songs to date. It is Weller does Garage Rock, and the speakers are filled with the sound of the album before we know what has hit us. The track, which ends up somewhere in the vein of the opening to the Stone Roses' second album, *Second Coming*, Breaking into Heaven, is enhanced perfectly from the programming and loops created by the Amorphous Androgynous (aka The Future Sound of London). The track is a real belter and gets the album going perfectly.

Although White Sky was the first new music heard from the album, track two, Saturns Pattern, the album's first single (or impact track), returns things to more familiar ground (as contemporary Weller albums are prone to), with a plodding drum sound, augmented by a huge chorus, a perfect showcase for where Weller's writing was currently at.

The album is huge, but is also stripped right back in terms of personnel, and aside from a bunch of regulars guesting here and there, most of *Saturns Pattern* is played by just the album's core musicians: Weller on vocals and guitar, Ben Gordelier (the kid who knocked on the studio door asking for some work experience) on drums, and Andy Crofts and co-producer Jan Kybert sharing bass and keyboard duties.

For the first time Weller chose to embrace studio production techniques fully on one of his albums, moving into the twenty-first century and bringing Pro-tools to Black Barn Studios. The digital technology allowed the famously erratic songwriter the opportunity of writing and recording sections of songs, and then moving them around on the computer, splicing them together to create whole tracks. The perfect example of this is track three, Going My Way, which is made up of a bunch of differently, seemingly unrelated, sections, all cut together, not unlike The Beatles' medley that makes up the second half of *Abbey Road*. But where the medley was created by a combination of smart musicianship and some poor studio engineer painstakingly cutting the tape together by hand, *Saturns Pattern* was created on the computer, with just a few clicks of the mouse.

This technique fit perfectly with the modern way that Weller liked top pen tracks by this point in his career: in the studio, rather than in his bedroom like he would have done in the old days. As Noel Gallagher says of the many times he has recorded with Weller, the process is not always that easy to comprehend:

> *I never go into the studio to just see what happens. But Paul is the opposite. Even though you think his songs are well*

structured and already written in the comfort of his home in front of the fire, they're not. Maybe in The Jam and Style Council days they were, but nowadays I think they're pretty much all written in the studio[xliii].

The end result is that *Saturns Pattern* is Weller's most current and vibrant album of the modern era. Alongside recapturing that soul sound – perfectly iterated in the album's simply incredible closing track, These City Streets – he mixes an array of styles that he loves, including the Stooges-alike Long Time, the wistful psychedelia of Pick It Up (one of just three tracks that Steve Craddock appears on), and the deep introspection of I'm Where I Should Be.

The new approach means the album has the energy and feel of a live record, all the tracks capturing the magic of having been recorded as they were being written, whilst simultaneously benefiting from the studio sheen and experimentation possible in the studio. The approach was (and is) very in vogue across pop music at the time, Ed Sheeran creating his albums mostly with electronic layers set against his acoustic guitar (meaning the musicians that appear can be counted on one hand), which also helps at bringing Weller's work up to date with the times, and the album's number 2 placing means it was clearly appealing to his audience.

As with all his albums though, Weller never forgets the most important thing: the song comes first. The sonorous melodies on *Saturns Pattern* could have been picked directly from the songbook of Motown in the sixties and are perfectly enhanced with the layers of lilting harmonies (courtesy of Wellers P. and H.), and that insistent driving rhythm (again, played by the young tea boy), creating as listenable a record as Weller has ever made.

Keep On Keeping On

With *Saturns Pattern* out in the world, by June 2015 Weller hopped across the pond to tour North America once again, taking in such cities as New York, Boston, Philad-elphia, Toronto, Chicago, Indianapolis, and Millvale (anyone?), before returning to play the world's most famous festival, Glastonbury on Sunday 28th June 2015. Despite appearing as special guest, playing ahead of Noel G., there are only really two acts in the world that Weller would play second to, one is Paul McCartney, and the other is The Who, the latter of whom headlined ahead of him in 2015, celebrating their fiftieth anniversary.

That same weekend Weller also headlined in Hyde Park, playing with Kaiser Chiefs and Johnny Marr, before hitting the road again, heading first to Spain, then Germany, Italy, Austria, Belgium, and once again to North America and then Japan, finishing the worldwide tour with a jaunt around the UK and Ireland.

In contrast, there were no gigs in 2016, and Weller was back in the studio writing and recording the soundtrack to *Jawbone*, and then an album of new material, *A Kind Revolution*, both of which were released in 2017.

Album 13:

A Kind Revolution
Released: 12th May 2017; UK Chart Position: 5; Label: Parlophone

Track Listing: Woo Sé Mama (Weller/Kybert); Nova; Long Long Road; She Moves with the Fayre; The Cranes are Back; Hopper; New York; One Tear (Weller/Kybert); Satellite Kid; The Impossible Idea
Producer/s: Paul Weller

UK Official Albums Chart – Top 10 – 19th May 2017:

1. *Harry Styles* – Harry Styles
2. ÷ – Ed Sheeran
3. *Human* – Rag'n'Bone Man
4. *After Laughter* – Paramore
5. ***A Kind Revolution* – Paul Weller**
6. *Common Sense* – J Hus
7. *For Crying Out Loud* – Kasabian
8. *More Life* – Drake
9. *Damn.* – Kendrick Lamar
10. *Life Love and Flesh Blood* – Imelda May

The albums chart in May 2017 was a real eclectic mix, with the undiluted pop of former One Direction front man Harry Styles, set amongst the Americana rock of Paramore, the sixth album from one of Britain's biggest and longest surviving contemporary rock bands Kasabian, as well as rappers Drake and the all-round prodigy Kendrick Lamar. The thing that seems to string all the artist together is that they all produce accessible pop music in their chosen genre.

And Weller is no different. *A Kind Revolution* was his thirteenth solo studio album, and you don't get to release that many albums (plus assorted live and best-ofs) without knowing how to connect with your audience.

A Kind Revolution

A four-star *Guardian* review called *A Kind Revolution*: "robustly written and emotionally satisfying"[xliv], whilst the *NME*, also going with four stars, called it "A textbook study in growing old gracefully"[xlv]. Both are bang on the mark, and it is easy to see why Weller went straight into recording *A Kind Revolution* after *Saturns Pattern*, knowing the muse was surging through him, and he wanted to get the songs down as quickly as he could.

However, far from being *Saturns Pattern* pt. 2, *A Kind Revolution* is a very different beast. Where *Saturns* is a confident thrash through genres and styles, and pieces of songs spliced together, its successor is much more considered. It takes its time, reaching its high points via a carefully plotted route, that becomes all the more enjoyable because of the journey.

That said, much the sound of the album is familiar to its predecessor in that it uses almost exactly the same personnel: his (and Cradock's) guitars are distorted and riff-laden, whilst Andy Crofts' Hammond and Philicorda, and semi-regular drummer Ben Gordelier, are all as prominent as is Jan Kybert's programming. Opening track Woo Sé Mama (Spanish, "Woo I Know Mama") is a jaunty, catchy pop track, that was released as a single in August 2017, and is aided by backing vocals from P.P. Arnold; whilst Nova (another single) attempts at futurism or perhaps psychedelia, by adding layers of bleeps and whirs courtesy of Crofts' Moog. Sadly, it sounds a little like the song's backing track is being played by nineties futurists Space.

Long Long Road, is a heartfelt ballad, with an acoustic guitar line familiar to Ocean Colour Scene's

1997 *Marchin' Already* album, but with an epic Small Faces-like chorus, that is about as good as anything from this whole period of Weller's career.

She Moves With the Fayre is another high-point, the band back on familiar ground with that blue-eyed soul sound it often feels like Weller invented, the stabbing guitars helped along by perfectly arranged strings, and a guest spot from the master of psychedelic rock, Robert Wyatt. Weller coaxed Wyatt out of retirement specifically for the album, and his vocal part appears just before an oddly placed, yet perfectly synchronous, Miles Davis-esque trumpet solo.

If there is a genre to *A Kind Revolution* then only Weller knows or cares what it is, and the album floats from track to track in a much more laid-back manner than its predecessor. A lazy critic could dismiss the album as the leftovers from *Saturns Pattern*, but to think that would be to miss the overall splendour and feel of the flow of the songs. The tracks are shorter and less adventurous musically then the previous album, but Weller's song writing is nothing but perfect, as always. There's the laid back bluesy-soul of The Cranes Are Back (complemented with angelic backing vocals from Steve Pilgrim), positioned next to the gentle melancholic strum of Hopper, a song inspired by the late American painter Edward Hopper, and his penchant for creating portraits of late night lonely figures in diners and bars ("the ghost of Hopper, paints such melancholy colours").

One Tear is a spaced-out epic builder, co-credited – because of its use of electronica – to Jan Kybert, and features Culture Club singer Boy George. Both George and Weller really push their vocal lines on his Chic-style funky-disco track, that lyrically demands responses to the biggest of questions ("If God is real, then show your face"), against layers of echo and reverb, before launching into a chorus about how damaging religion can be: "I don't want your kinds of gods, that divide us". It's ambitious stuff (and likely to receive a backlash), and much like the rest of the album finds Weller and his band in yet another completely individual space.

Another Jaunt Round the Islands

The rest of 2017 disappeared in a blur of live dates, which firstly took in the British Isles, before heading off into the mainland (now separating, in mind if not yet spirit, from the UK thanks to the June 2016 vote to leave the EU), and those ever faithful Germans, and then on to Belgium, The Netherlands, Austria, Italy, Spain etc. etc. etc. heading around the world into 2018, to Japan, Australia, and then back to the UK in order to record *True Meanings*, in time for a September 2018 release.

Album 14:

True Meanings
Released: 14th September 2018; UK Chart Position: 2; Label: Parlophone
Track Listing: The Soul Searchers (Weller/O'Brien); Glide; Mayfly; Gravity; Old Castles; What Would He Say?; Aspects; Bowie (Weller/Cooper): Wishing Well; Come Along; Books; Movin' On (Weller/Brown/Doyle); May Love Travel With You; White Horses (Weller/Cooper)
Producer/s: Paul Weller

UK Official Albums Chart – Top 10 – 21st September 2018:

1. *Kamikaze* – Eminem
2. ***True Meanings* – Paul Weller**
3. *The Greatest Showman* – OST and Cast Recording
4. *Mama Mia – Here We Go Again* – OST and Cast Recording
5. *Sweetener* – Ariana Grande
6. *Staying at Tamara's* – George Ezra
7. *Scorpion* – Drake
8. *My Mind Makes Noises* – Pale Waves
9. *7* – David Guetta
10. *For Ever* – Jungle

Losing out on the top spot to one of the biggest hitters of the twenty-first century, Eminem, and his comeback album *Kamikaze*, was not the end of the world for Weller. Particularly because of the downbeat, acoustic nature of *True Meanings*, compared to the in-your-face-ness of *Kamikaze*.

Eminem's UK chart success is phenomenal, with nine of the rappers ten studio albums hitting the top spot between 2000 and 2020. To date he has amassed 11 top 10 albums (alongside his debut which reached number 10, and a Greatest Hits, which also reached number 1), and ten number 1 singles, in a career spanning more than 20 years.

True Meanings

Weller's fourteenth studio album returns the aging rocker to the style and tone of his early nineties *Wild Wood* phase, and every one of 14 tracks is played on the acoustic guitar, with just a spattering of outside accompaniment. Led by the beautiful opening track The Soul Searchers, co-written by Conor O'Brien from

The Villagers, the album announces itself as a much gentler and more heartfelt affair than we have seen from Weller for some time. Although he is no strange to pouring his heart out via his more up-tempo numbers, Weller has a way of expressing himself via the simplistic poignancy of the acoustic that hits the spot perfectly.

True Meanings pressed the pause button on the studio experimentation of *Saturns Pattern* and the full band set up of *A Kind Revolution*, and started a whole new, more reflective phase, that has continued into *On Sunset* and *Fat Pop*.

If we didn't already know that Weller's albums of the new decade were genre defying, then the word 'folk' would come up a lot when talking about *True Meanings*. And folk is certainly one way to look at the album, with the singer tapping into his deepest inner Woody Guthrie or Joan Baez on The Soul Searchers and Glide, whilst Mayfly begins with a T-Rex-esque guitar lick, then lifts part of the melody of Sunflower from *Wild Wood*, before leading off in a brass-led soul-like direction for its chorus. Despite this erratic mixing of genres (again), it is one of the high-lights of the album and vies for the accolade of one of the best tracks of this whole period.

Gravity is a simple acoustic track, supplemented with rich, lustrous strings, and harmony vocals, that wouldn't be out of place in a West End musical, and is not unlike On The Street Where You Live from *My Fair Lady* ("In my heart you'll always be, the greatest love that I could feel"). This feeling is continued into Old Castles, whilst What Would He Say? returns its writer to a thoughtful, imagined lyric about how long dead relatives might view current actions from beyond the grave. With John Weller nearly ten years gone by this point, it isn't hard to think who Paul might have been thinking about when he penned the track.

Once again drawing on *This is Spinal Tap*, in Rob Reiner's 1984 cult classic, the band present the idea of an acoustic album as something of a joke, self-indulgent and overly stodgy for fans, but if you've got as much longevity as Paul Weller, the exact opposite can also be true. By 2018, Weller was exactly forty years into his musical career, and 26 years a solo artist, and he had earned himself the right to take a look back at his life – so intrinsically wrapped up with his musical journey – and the long, rambling story that got him to where he was forty years later.

The title *True Meanings* suggests that Weller is finally able to look back on with some form of objectivity, considering the past and what it all means – it's, true meaning – from the safety and strength of his present. Bowie, a simple ode to the great man (although it could also be about his son…), tragically lost in 2016 ("How can the world lose his name?"), is again just Weller and his acoustic (and those strings, perhaps a little too overpowering), as is Wishing Well (thankfully free of those strings), and Come Along, and the whole album becomes a tribute to the simple art of song writing itself. Inspirations are typically prominent though, and alongside the general touch stones of Lennon/McCartney, Marriot, Lane, can be added the likes of Bowie, Dylan and even an Indian influence (on the George Harrison-esque, Books), which includes sitar and tampoura, played by Sheema Murkajee.

The album's real strength comes from how much Weller can achieve with so little, a real testament to less-is-more. After two albums that were nine and ten tracks long, but were noted for their marked attempts at experimentation, the 14 tracks on *True*

Meanings, could quite easily have meant the album lagged, particularly because of its spared down nature. But the variation between tracks is incredibly well handled, showing the real skill Weller shows at the simplistic nature of acoustic music.

Movin' On signals the album is coming to a close, and the song could not be more aptly named if it had been called, So, What's Next?, written with Tom Doyle and Anth Brown (known together as White Label), the track is one of the few moments where the album lifts above the gentle, and Doyle even gets the chance to add some drums. White Label may have cowritten the song, but the sentiment summed up in its key line is all Weller: "I got love all around, I don't need nothing", and it starts to bring to end a very interesting and introspective album. One of his best of the modern era.

Other Aspects – Live at the Royal Festival Hall

Instead of heading out on yet another lengthy tour, a month after the release of *True Meanings*, Weller appeared live at the Royal Festival Hall in London's Southbank Centre for two special concerts. It would be the only concerts he would play in support of the new album and would be his last time playing live for nearly a year. Luckily for everyone who attended, something quite special happened on those nights.

With material mostly comprised of the *True Meanings* album, Weller's guitar and piano were backed by Steve Cradock, Andy Crofts, Steve Pilgrim, Tom Heel and Ben Gordelier, and for the first time, the London Metropolitan Orchestra. It was the perfect way to exhibit the new album, and the likes of The Soul Searchers and Mayfly were interspersed with the odd classic like Wild Wood and You Do Something to Me.

The whole idea was to move away from the rock 'n' roll side of Weller's live style, and he worked hard at showcasing how well he could do with a full orchestra behind him. The concert went down so well that it was released in March 2019 as a x3 LP album and DVD called *Other Aspects – Live at the Royal Festival Hall.*

Live Album 5:

Other Aspects – Live at the Royal Festival Hall
Released: 8th March 2019; UK Chart Position: 10; Label: Parlophone
Track Listing: LP1: One Bright Star (Weller/Dine); Glide; The Soul Searchers (Weller/O'Brien); Boy About Town; Have You Ever Had It Blue; What Would He Say?; Wild Wood; Country
LP2: Aspects; Strange Museum (Weller/Talbot); Amongst Butterflies; Old Castles; Gravity; Where'er Ye Go; A Man of Great Promise; Mayfly; Private Hell
LP3: Tales From the Riverbank; Movin On (Anth Brown); Long Long Road; Hopper; White Horses (Erland Cooper); Books (Weller/Tom Doyle); You Do Something to Me; May Love Travel With You
Producer/s: various

UK Official Albums Chart – Top 10 – 15th March 2019:

1. *Psychodrama* – Dave
2. *Everything Not Saved Will Be Lost – Part 1* – Foals
3. *Still on My Mind* – Dido

4. *Sucker Punch* – Sigrid
5. *What a Time to be Alive* – Tom Walker
6. *The Greatest Showman* – OST and Cast Recording
7. *Bohemian Rhapsody* – OST – Queen
8. *Thanks U Next* – Ariana Grande
9. *Staying at Tamara's* – George Ezra
10. ***Other Aspects – Live at the Royal Festival Hall* – Paul Weller**

A high chart placing for a live album, particularly one mostly composed of tracks from an album released just six months earlier, *Other Aspects – Live at the Royal Festival Hall*, showed that there was still a lot of interest in Weller, particularly when presenting his music in different ways.

At the top spot in March 2019 was the Mercury Prize winning debut from Dave, *Psychodrama*, an album that is loosely composed around the theme of mental health awareness (hence the title). The candid nature of Dave's warts-and-all tales of darkness and depression mean there is a graphic honesty to the album that pushes it to the extremes of pop music. It said a lot about the UK record buying public that *Psychodrama* went to the number 1 the same week that the soundtracks to *The Greatest Showman* and *Bohemian Rhapsody* were in the top 10.

CHAPTER TEN
Weller Under Lockdown – *On Sunset* and *Fat Pop (Volume 1)* (2020-2021)

Paul Weller played his last gig before lockdown was announced in the UK, the night before, at the Olympia Theatre in Dublin, on Sunday 22nd March 2020. There is no doubting that locking the country down was the correct measure to ensure COVID-19 stopped spreading at such an alarming rate, but not being able to play live was unnerving for Weller as an artist. Playing live is where he really stretches his legs as a musician, honing his craft, and connecting one to one with his audience, working out what does and doesn't work in a song by his crowd's reaction to it. There was the concern that he would lose touch with his audience if he couldn't play live. Luckily for him and his fans, this wouldn't be the case.

Saving lives is the most important thing, but the entertainment industry was one of the hardest hit by the COVID-19 pandemic. Weller may have been unable to connect with his audience in the way he would have liked, but lockdown did give him the opportunity of focusing on the other side of his life as a musician, recording. If only he had a studio at the end of his garden… Well, not quite, he bought Black Barn Studios back in 1999, and even though he split his time between his house in Central London and Surrey, he and his family locked themselves down in the cottage adjacent to the studio, and the various members of his band soon began to receive ideas for songs popping up in their inboxes.

Locked Down in the Studio

Before this though, there was the small matter of putting out the album he had already recorded before lockdown. His fifteenth studio album *On Sunset* was ready for release in March 2020, and due to the pandemic, Weller was forced to cancel a whole tour he had planned to promote the album. It was quite the deadly blow, and Weller rightly worried that it would finally put an end to the incredible streak he had been on over the last decade.

As history tells us, it didn't put an end to anything, and like many others, Weller survived by adapting and soon entered into the spirit of lockdown by presenting 'Mid-Sömmer Musik', recorded in July, but released on 12th November, an hour-long live stream so his audience could stay in touch, and even hear new material. Then, with little else to do, and certainly not one to mope, he began to write again, and soon channelled his concentration into another album. *Fat Pop (Volume 1)* was released less than a year after *On Sunset*, in May 2021.

Since then, he has been happily back out on the road to support the album, and on 15th May 2021, he played another huge live concert at the London Barbican, but with no audience, this time backed by the BBC Symphony Orchestra, playing some of his most loved compositions, with special arrangements by Jules Buckley. The likes of Broken Stones and English Rose are set amidst tracks from *On Sunset* and *Fat Pop*, and *An Orchestrated Songbook* is set to be released on 3rd December 2021.

Album 15:

On Sunset
Released: 3rd July 2020; UK Chart Position: 1;
Label: Polydor
Track Listing: Mirror Ball; Baptiste; Old Father Time; Village (Weller/Kybert); More; On Sunset; Equanimity; Walkin'; Earth Beat (Weller/Cole Basta/Jim Jupp); Rockets
Producer/s: Paul Weller; Jan Kybert

UK Official Albums Chart – Top 10 – 10th July 2020:

1. ***On Sunset* – Paul Weller**
2. *Shoot for the Stars Aim for the Moon* – Pop Smoke
3. *Cinema Paradiso* – Katherine Jenkins
4. *Divinely Uninspired to a Hellish Extent* – Lewis Capaldi
5. *Rough and Rowdy Ways* – Bob Dylan
6. *Fine Lines* – Harry Styles
7. *A Steady Drip Drip Drip* – Sparks
8. *Chromatica* – Lady Gaga
9. *Future Nostalgia* – Dua Lipa
10. *Cannibal* – Bury Tomorrow

Originally planned for release on 12th June, but kept back because of the pandemic, *On Sunset* went straight into the chart at the top spot, awarding Weller his fifth UK number 1 album. He tops a chart comprised of an eclectic mix of newer artists like Harry Styles, Lewis Capaldi and Dua Lipa (an eclectic mix just themselves), plus some older favourites like Lady Gaga and Katherine Jenkins, and a few legends like Sparks, and even the very well received new album from Bob Dylan. There is even a place for the vastly different styles of US rapper Pop Smoke, and metalcore band Bury Tomorrow.

On Sunset

Despite being written and recorded before lockdown, *On Sunset* appeared in the milieu surrounding the first phase of the pandemic, and by chance rather than design, gains its distinct identity as album because of its association to the crazy changing time. Weller was planning a live show around it, but *On Sunset* is definitely a studio album, and his classic approach to song writing was now perfectly augmented by cutting and pasting segments of songs into place to create a full track. Where once he would have used strings, epic opening track Mirror Ball is weighted with layers of keyboards and programming (courtesy of our old friend Jan Kybert), adding a sense of drama and futurism once the full band crashes in, and the track takes off in a totally different direction.

Of course, the guitars of course still lead the charge, this is after all a Paul Weller album, and Weller and Steve Cradock's Epiphones and Les Pauls spit out hooks and riffs on top of and alongside Kybert's programming in perfect synchronicity. Since around the time of *Illumination* in 2002, writing songs in the studio had become Weller's preferred way of writing, and since 2015's *Saturns Pattern*, using Pro-tools to splice together sections of tracks had allowed an even more organic process of authorship. *On Sunset* is pitched perfectly into that comfortable space between writing a song and recording it, when it still sounds new and vibrant and exciting for the band to play.

It's not all whirrs and beeps though, and for every moment of programming, there are two of mellotron, saxophone and beautifully layered soulful backing vocals, such as the old soul sound of Baptiste, or the funky mix of the old and the new in Old Father Tyme, an ode to mortality told with beautiful poetry, not unlike Wilde's *Picture of Dorian Gray*:

Like those tired branches
On that old oak tree
Strange beauty in winter
But how sweeter in spring

In stark contrast to Old Father Tyme is the album's second single Village, as straight-forward pop as the album gets, a mid-tempo number with a hummable chorus about how contented with his life Weller is: "Not a thing I'd change if I could, I'm happy here in my neighbourhood". Showing his experience as an artist, on an album noted for its musical experimentation, Weller knows when to pull back, and the song is kept simple, allowed to speak for itself.

Like most of his albums at this point in his career, if there is a theme to *On Sunset*, it is about Weller looking around at his life and gently considering what has come before, and what is currently there in front of him. So confident is he in his abilities as a musician, that he is happy to dip into musical genres, plucking pieces for redistribution at the right moment. The melodies live and breathe, rising and falling like old Motown classics and modern soulful masters, of which he is clearly one, and the album takes its time in gently letting itself unfold. More, a track complimented by a verse from French singer Stella Page, even has a long jazz-style outro filled with oboes and flutes alongside the guitars and strings, yet still manages to anchor itself to the Weller-sound; whilst the honky tonk piano is given an outing on Equanimity, and Walkin', in a similar vein, wouldn't have sounded out of place in a vaudeville music hall during the thirties and forties.

Despite his continued journey into the folds of what programming and computers can do to help support the song, Weller is still at his best strumming his acoustic, backed by drums, bass and guitars, like on the title track, on which the song is once again given its own space to breath. That said, the album's strongest track might be Earth Beat, the first single, which sounds so different to everything else that Weller has done. The song channels new wave and electronica alongside classic R&B pop, the synths positioned right at the top of the mix, overpowering the subtle guitar lines, and the whole song is washed with backing vocals from The Staves, and all girl indie-folk group, who really help define the best of the song.

In any other hands, Earth Beat may have set the wrong tone for the album, which although heavy with musical experimentation, is not defined by it. But then no other artist would have produced Earth Beat, and Weller is careful to place it at the end of the short 10 track album (although it was the first single), the final track returning him to his acoustic guitar, and the gentle melancholia of Rockets. It's shame that he never got to fully tour *On Sunset*. That would have been some show.

More Music Locked Down

Album 16:

Fat Pop (Volume 1)
Released: 14th May 2021; UK Chart Position: 1; Label: Polydor
Track Listing: Cosmic Fingers; True (Weller/Lia Metcalfe); Fat Pop (Weller/Kybert); Shades of Blue (P. Weller/Leah Weller); Glad Times (Weller/Brown/Doyle); Cobweb/ Connections; Testify (Weller/Andy Fairweather-Low); That Pleasure; Failed; Moving Canvas; In Better Times; Still Glides The Stream (Weller/Cradock)
Producer/s: Paul Weller; Jan Kybert

UK Official Albums Chart – Top 10 – 21st May 2021:

1. ***Fat Pop (Volume 1)* – Paul Weller**
2. *The Off-Season* – J. Cole
3. *Life by Misadventure* – Rag'n'Bone Man
4. *Daddy's Home* – St. Vincent
5. *Delta Kream* – Black Keys
6. *Future Nostalgia* – Dua Lipa
7. *The Highlights* – Weeknd
8. *Diamonds* – Elton John
9. *Be Right Back* – Jorja Smith
10. *We Are More Than One* – Michael Ball

Weller's second album within 12 months, *Fat Pop (Volume 1)* had no less impact than its predecessor *On Sunset*, but found Weller still at the top of his game, and the top of his popularity. His sixth number 1, and sixteenth top 10 album, *Fat Pop* continued his run of successful studio albums, hanging around in the chart for six weeks.

Not quite as divisive as the chart back in July 2020, the top 10 in May 2021 was also filled with artists who had recorded under lockdown, notably Rag'n'Bone Man, and his second number 1 album *Life by Misadventure*, plus pop-soulstress St Vincent's biggest UK release *Daddy's Home*, and the second album after an extended five years break from blues-rockers Black Keys, *Delta Kream*.

The likes of Elton John sitting alongside The Weeknd continue the eclecticism that we have come to expect in the charts in 2021; and just outside the top 10, at number 11, is *Queen's Greatest Hits I*, officially the UK's biggest selling album of all time, continuing its mega run of 946 weeks in the UK Albums Chart. In a little over a year, the album will likely join ABBA's *Gold* collection, as only the second album ever to run for 1000 weeks on the chart (achieved in July 2021)[xlvi].

Fat Pop (Volume 1)

With no touring allowed, Weller was awarded the acclaim of guest editor of *Mojo* magazine for the June 2021 issue (released in May), just as his new album was released. As he told Ted Kessler (the former *NME* journo that had called *Stanley Road*, "doggedly retro"), the plan with *Fat Pop (Volume 1)* – the 'volume 1' leaving the field open either for a follow up, or perhaps even a new franchise (ever forward thinking) – was to make an album "where every song could be released as a single".

Despite singles no longer being released from albums ("they call them 'impact tracks' now," as Weller mournfully told Kessler), *Fat Pop* landed not far away from its ambitious intention. If *On Sunset* was marked for returning Weller to the world of musical experimentation, then its aptly named successor is the "all-new 12-song burst of three-minute knee-tremblers"[xlvii] that Kessler described it as.

Opener Cosmic Fringes is a partly tongue-in-cheek track, and a not too distant cousin of Squeeze's Up the Junction, that kicks the album off with some nifty drum programming from engineer Charles Rees, the only other musician (other than Cradock) who appears on the song. The album still includes the cast of thousands we are familiar with from all contemporary Weller records (they mostly emailed over their parts, or recorded them between lock downs), Weller is just letting us know, as the album gets going, the mostly solitary environment in which it was created. Expressing himself the best way he can, through his music.

Once again offering a helping hand to newer artists, track two features a co-lead vocal by Lia Metcalfe from up and coming Liverpool outfit The Mysterines, who also gets a writing credit (lock down must have been extra tough on those bands posed to break it at that exact moment), and the track is classic Weller indie-rock.

The one-two hit of Fat Pop and first single (sorry, impact track...) Shades of Blue, properly gets the album going, and the two tracks sit at the heart of what *Fat Pop* says as an album. The former, an ode to pop music itself ("Who's always there when your life is down?"), is Weller as played by Gorillaz, complete with Damon Albarn-style melodica, and synths by Tom Heel; whilst the latter, co-written with Weller's oldest daughter Leah, is a piano-led, up-beat trooper of a track with a very pleasing chord drop before the anthemic chorus. Perhaps because Leah helped write it, but the track is quite unlike anything Weller had done before, showing us that he can still surprise even 45 years into his recording career.

Glad Times (written with White Label), takes on a more mournful tone, and tackles as its subject matter the insecurities that we all feel as adults, but had assumed that someone like Weller never did. Only too happy to humanise himself on record, age has brought with it a kind of introspective honesty to Weller's albums, first properly acknowledged in *True Meanings*, and continued onto *On Sunset* and inevitably, *Fat Pop*. The self-reflection is tantamount, and on tracks like Glad Times and the deeply personal Failed, he lets the lyrics lead the feel of the track, so gauging the overall tone of the album.

The mix of genres is as evident as ever, and the acoustic folky protest feel of Testify, leaps to the blissed out contemporary soul of That Pleasure, a track that just drips with beautiful orchestration, and wouldn't have sounded out of place on a late period Marvin Gaye album.

The album didn't completely impress everyone, *The Guardian*, usually on side with Weller's changing sounds, called it "an album that's ultimately more earnest than exciting" in a lower than par three-star review. Although they did call closing track, the brilliantly named Still Glides the Stream "a classy slice of stately, reflective chamber pop"[xlviii]. A statement that coolly predicates Weller's instinctual next move toward playing with the BBC Symphony Orchestra on the *An Orchestrated Songbook* album. As it looks to be, the perfect next move for an artist deeply imbedded into the solo phase of his musical journey.

An Instinctual Ride

Instincts have played a key part in Weller's continued success, and his natural reaction to the global pandemic was to produce an album of (fat) pop songs. The album may at first glance appear more light weight than much of his recent output, but on closer inspection, it doesn't shy away from engaging with darker personal subject matter. *Fat Pop* embraces its themes of insecurity and the fear of failure – feelings that many people would have struggled to escape from amid the lack of ambient background noise of lockdown – as something of a beacon, positioning the author as a bright focal point and example for many. *True Meanings* wouldn't have worked as well in 2020 or 2021, because it was too abjectly mournful for that moment. Upbeat pop music was right for the time, but as Weller teaches us, such music doesn't need to be disposable.

Which of course strikes at the heart of what makes Weller such a fascinating song writer. The general criticism levelled at him is that he is an everyman artist, and this is completely true, but trying to position this as a criticism is to miss out on the importance of such a role. Many of the greatest artists of all time have been 'the everyman', John Lennon, for example. In the last decade of his life, Lennon was an artist at once distanced by immense wealth and stature, but who was still happy to be seen as the stay at home dad, or dressed in his ex-army combats, protesting in the street against the Vietnam War. And Paul Weller feels much closer to the man in the street than Lennon. You could imagine bumping into him in the Nags Head (having an OJ), and he would be just as happy posing for a selfie as he would discussing the lyrically themes of his latest album.

Where an artist like Noel Gallagher is inconsistent with portraying his feelings or sense of self lyrically, Weller has learned over the course of 45 years as a recording artist to trust his instincts, and place his feelings front and centre, whatever they might be. Which in turn normalises talking about how you feel, for a sub-section of people (middle-aged men), notoriously bad at that.

Back in the late seventies he wrote about what he saw around him, "A smash of glass and the rumble of boots" and "Headlines of death and sorrow, they tell of tomorrow", of paranoia and conflict in a temperamental, changing society. And writing so honestly helped his audience identify with him. In his second incarnation, as one half of the haughtily named The Style Council, he tried to turn the view point inwards, but ended up either becoming overly sentimental, "I've had my share of life's ups and downs, But fate's been kind, the downs have been few", or overly banal, "What once was pleasure, now's pain for us all, I once stood proud, now I feel so small".

It took him a few goes, but once his solo career got started, he slowly learned to let the barriers down and release whatever it was he was feeling, positive or negative, onto the page. What began as the elusive feel of Into Tomorrow, "Buy a dream and hideaway... As we head into tomorrow", slowly morphed into the beautifully crafted imagery of Wild Wood, the perfect metaphor for his densely packed state of mind, "Climbing, forever trying, to find your way out of the wild, wild wood."

By the time he hit his imperial phase with the double tap success of *Stanley Road* and *Heavy Soul* he was able to offer an air of nostalgia and self-reference, that chimed just perfectly with his audience, who by then were aging along with him; whilst gathering a whole host of new listeners as he went. This meant that in the mid-late nineties, he was in the enviable position of being both a relatively new artist, who was also incredibly experienced at the same time; plus the time was right for rock 'n' roll again, and the big bands of the day, both Blur and Oasis, cited his past and present work as key influences on themselves.

Acts like Weller, Noel Gallagher, Damon Albarn, as well as Johnny Marr, Radiohead, even Coldplay, make longevity look easy, yet it is anything but. Updating and changing your style of writing, playing and recording, whilst maintaining your original sense of integrity, is a huge challenge, but Weller has made it look effortless, mostly because he has only become more aware of who he is as a song writer, and as an artist, the older he has got. Many think he is trapped in the sixties, amid the ironically named Modernist movement (modern, up until 1970), and there is no doubting that he is indeed King Mod, but just listen to the samples and programming on Mirror Ball, or the folky acoustic reflection on *True Meanings*. He changes and updates his style and sound because he is a fan of music, and is constantly listening to new and interesting artists, who release new and interesting music.

We are nothing but a sum total of our experiences, and by keeping his head in the game, aware of the changing trends and movements, Paul Weller has always managed to remain the most critical of British musical artists.

What Next for the Modfather?

As Weller said to Ted Kessler in that June 2021 *Mojo*, "If we don't gig until 2022, I'll be 64 that year. That's a funny old age to go back on the road." But go back on the road he undoubtably will, and record new music and release excellent new albums that manage to be cemented in the past whilst simultaneously somehow pushing modern music forwards at the same time, he will also do. Chiefly because that's what he does, and he doesn't know any different. As Steve Cradock says, "He's been on the road since the 1970s", how on earth could that change?

Of course, the day will come when he has to retire from playing live concerts. Perhaps he'll slowly step back, appearing just once a year, and then once every two or three years at his beloved Royal Albert Hall, and then, like Leonard Cohen before him, he'll make a record every few years. But, this is not that day, and it won't be for quite some time. We have plenty of live performances left to look forward to, and if the run of albums of late have been anything to go by, plenty of staggeringly good new music to listen to as well. Long live the Modfather.

THE END

ABOUT THE AUTHOR

Tom Boniface-Webb is a writer and sometime filmmaker from Reading in the South-East of the United Kingdom. He currently lives in Wellington, New Zealand with his wife Donna and their two daughters, Isabelle and Abigail.

In 2017 his first non-fiction book 'I Was Britpopped: The A-Z of Britpop' was published through Valley Press, written with the co-author Jenny Natasha. First published in October 2020, there are seven entries to the Modern Music Masters series and counting. Feel free to get in touch if you would like to pitch an entry to the series.

For more information about the Modern Music Masters series:
modernmusicmastersuk@gmail.com

End Notes

---

[i] Mojo, no. 331, June 2021
[ii] 'Paul Weller: Sounds from the Studio' by Ian Snowball, This Day in Music Books (2020), pgs. 132-133
[iii] 'Paul Weller: Sounds from the Studio' by Ian Snowball, This Day in Music Books (2020), pgs. 133
[iv] All Weller tour dates quoted from - https://www.songkick.com/artists/398255-paul-weller/gigography
[v] 'Paul Weller: Sounds from the Studio' by Ian Snowball, This Day in Music Books (2020), locs. 1972
[vi] 'Paul Weller – The Changing Man' by Paulo Hewitt, Penguin (2011), locs. 2589
[vii] Source - https://www.theguardian.com/music/2021/nov/25/paul-wellers-30-greatest-songs-ranked?CMP=Share_iOSApp_Other
[viii] 'Paul Weller: Sounds from the Studio' by Ian Snowball, This Day in Music Books (2020), locs. 2023
[ix] Source - https://web.archive.org/web/20000930045151/http://www.nme.com/reviews/reviews/19980101000686reviews.html
[x] Source - https://web.archive.org/web/20000930045151/http://www.nme.com/reviews/reviews/19980101000686reviews.html
[xi] Source - https://www.theguardian.com/music/2021/nov/25/paul-wellers-30-greatest-songs-ranked?CMP=Share_iOSApp_Other
[xii] Mojo, no. 332, July 2021
[xiii] BPI - https://www.bpi.co.uk/brit-certified/
[xiv] Blur released *Modern Life is Rubbish* (1993), *Parklife* (1994) and *The Great Escape* (1995); whilst Oasis released *Definitely Maybe* (1994), *(What's the Story) Morning Glory?* [1995], and *Be Here Now* (1997)
[xv] BPI - https://www.bpi.co.uk/brit-certified/
[xvi] BPI - https://www.bpi.co.uk/brit-certified/
[xvii] BPI - https://www.bpi.co.uk/brit-certified/
[xviii] Stats from *NME*, dated 26th August 1995
[xix] Ref -

https://web.archive.org/web/20150919014912/http://www.bpi.co.uk/assets/files/Yearly%20best%20sellers%20-%20albums.pdf

[xx] Ref - https://www.theguardian.com/friday_review/story/0,,178308,00.html

[xxi] 'Paul Weller: Sounds from the Studio' by Ian Snowball, This Day in Music Books (2020), pg. 85

[xxii] 'Paul Weller: Sounds from the Studio' by Ian Snowball, This Day in Music Books (2020), pg. 85

[xxiii] BPI - https://www.bpi.co.uk/brit-certified/

[xxiv] As at time of writing – 02/11/21

[xxv] BPI - https://www.bpi.co.uk/brit-certified/

[xxvi] BPI - https://www.bpi.co.uk/brit-certified/

[xxvii] BPI - https://www.bpi.co.uk/brit-certified/

[xxviii] Source - https://twitter.com/jamesblunt/status/808599054989070336?lang=en

[xxix] BPI - https://www.bpi.co.uk/brit-certified/

[xxx] 'Paul Weller: Sounds from the Studio' by Ian Snowball, This Day in Music Books (2020), pg. 66

[xxxi] 'Paul Weller: Sounds from the Studio' by Ian Snowball, This Day in Music Books (2020), locs. 1072

[xxxii] Source - https://www.bbc.com/news/entertainment-arts-49008689

[xxxiii] 'Paul Weller: Sounds from the Studio' by Ian Snowball, This Day in Music Books (2020), locs. 882

[xxxiv] 'Paul Weller: Sounds from the Studio' by Ian Snowball, This Day in Music Books (2020), pg. 46

[xxxv] Source - https://www.bpi.co.uk/brit-certified/

[xxxvi] Source - https://freeyourmusic.com/blog/how-much-does-spotify-pay-per-stream

[xxxvii] Source - https://www.theguardian.com/music/2021/apr/20/paul-mccartney-kate-bush-law-change-music-streaming-payment?CMP=Share_iOSApp_Other

[xxxviii] Source - https://www.theguardian.com/music/2021/apr/20/paul-mccartney-kate-bush-law-change-music-streaming-payment?CMP=Share_iOSApp_Other

xxxix As at time of writing – 04/11/2021

xl BPI - https://www.bpi.co.uk/brit-certified/

xli 'Paul Weller: Sounds from the Studio' by Ian Snowball, This Day in Music Books (2020), locs. 613

xlii 'Paul Weller: Sounds from the Studio' by Ian Snowball, This Day in Music Books (2020), locs. 279

xliii 'Paul Weller: Sounds from the Studio' by Ian Snowball, This Day in Music Books (2020), locs. 448

xliv Source - https://www.theguardian.com/music/2017/may/11/paul-weller-a-kind-revolution-review-robustly-written-and-emotionally-satisfying

xlv Source - https://www.nme.com/reviews/paul-weller-kind-revolution-review-2069220

xlvi Source - https://www.officialcharts.com/chart-news/abba-gold-becomes-first-album-to-reach-1000-weeks-on-the-official-albums-chart__33502/

xlvii All refs in this paragraph from Mojo, no. 331, June 2021

xlviii Source - https://www.theguardian.com/music/2021/may/16/paul-weller-fat-pop-volume-1-one-review

Printed in Great Britain
by Amazon

72179241R00119